Praise for *Essential Skills for the Agile Developer*

"I tell teams that the lean and agile practices should be treated like a buffet: Don't try and take everything, or it will make you ill—try the things that make sense for your project. In this book the authors have succinctly described the 'why' and the 'how' of some of the most effective practices, enabling all software engineers to write quality code for short iterations in an efficient manner."

—Kay Johnson
Software Development Effectiveness Consultant, IBM

"Successful agile development requires much more than simply mastering a computer language. It requires a deeper understanding of agile development methodologies and best practices. *Essential Skills for the Agile Developer* provides the perfect foundation for not only learning but truly understanding the methods and motivations behind agile development."

—R.L. Bogetti
www.RLBogetti.com,
Lead System Designer, Baxter Healthcare

"*Essential Skills for the Agile Developer* is an excellent resource filled with practical coding examples that demonstrate key agile practices."

—Dave Hendricksen
Software Architect, Thomson Reuters

The Net Objectives Lean-Agile Series

Alan Shalloway, Series Editor

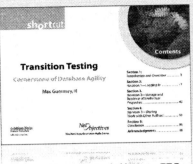

Visit **informit.com/netobjectives** for a complete list of available publications.

The **Net Objectives Lean-Agile Series** provides fully integrated Lean-Agile training, consulting, and coaching solutions for businesses, management, teams, and individuals. Series editor Alan Shalloway and the Net Objectives team strongly believe that it is not the software, but rather the value that software contributes—to the business, to the consumer, to the user—that is most important.

The best—and perhaps only—way to achieve effective product development across an organization is a well-thought-out combination of Lean principles to guide the enterprise, agile practices to manage teams, and core technical skills. The goal of **The Net Objectives Lean-Agile Series** is to establish software development as a true profession while helping unite management and individuals in work efforts that "optimize the whole," including

- The whole organization: Unifying enterprises, teams, and individuals to best work together
- The whole product: Not just its development, but also its maintenance and integration
- The whole of time: Not just now, but in the future—resulting in a sustainable return on investment

The books included in this series are written by expert members of Net Objectives. These books are designed to help practitioners understand and implement the key concepts and principles that drive the development of valuable software.

PEARSON

✦Addison-Wesley **Cisco Press** EXAM/**CRAM** **IBM** Press. **QUE** ⠿ PRENTICE HALL **SAMS** | Safari›

Essential Skills for the
Agile Developer

Essential Skills for the Agile Developer

A Guide to Better Programming and Design

Alan Shalloway
Scott Bain
Ken Pugh
Amir Kolsky

✦✦Addison-Wesley

Upper Saddle River, NJ • Boston • Indianapolis • San Francisco
New York • Toronto • Montreal • London • Munich • Paris • Madrid
Capetown • Sydney • Tokyo • Singapore • Mexico City

Many of the designations used by manufacturers and sellers to distinguish their products are claimed as trademarks. Where those designations appear in this book, and the publisher was aware of a trademark claim, the designations have been printed with initial capital letters or in all capitals.

The authors and publisher have taken care in the preparation of this book, but make no expressed or implied warranty of any kind and assume no responsibility for errors or omissions. No liability is assumed for incidental or consequential damages in connection with or arising out of the use of the information or programs contained herein.

The publisher offers excellent discounts on this book when ordered in quantity for bulk purchases or special sales, which may include electronic versions and/or custom covers and content particular to your business, training goals, marketing focus, and branding interests. For more information, please contact:

U.S. Corporate and Government Sales
(800) 382-3419
corpsales@pearsontechgroup.com

For sales outside the United States please contact:

International Sales
international@pearson.com

Visit us on the Web: informit.com/aw

Library of Congress Cataloging-in-Publication Data
Essential skills for the agile developer : a guide to better programming and design / Alan Shalloway . . . [et al.].
        p.   cm.
    Includes index.
    ISBN 978-0-321-54373-8 (pbk. : alk. paper)
  1. Agile software development. I. Shalloway, Alan.
    QA76.76.D47E74 2011
    005.1—dc23
                                                                2011023686

ISBN-13: 978-0-321-54373-8
ISBN-10:   0-321-54373-4
This product is printed digitally on demand.

First Printing: August 2011 with corrections made August 2013

To my loving and lifetime partner, Leigh, my muse, who keeps me more humble than I would otherwise be. And while giving me a reason not to be writing books, keeps the pressure up to get the job done.

—Alan Shalloway

To June Carol Bain. I wish she had lived to see her son become the teacher she always told him he should be. Hey, mom, you nailed it.

—Scott Bain

To Ron, Shelly, and Maria: those who matter.

—Amir Kolsky

To my brother Don, who gave me a reason to become an engineer.

—Ken Pugh

Contents

Chapter 5
Encapsulate That! _____ 53

Chapter 6
Interface-Oriented Design _____ 75

Chapter 9
Continuous Integration

Part III
Design Issues

Chapter 10
Commonality and Variability Analysis

Chapter 11
Refactor to the Open-Closed

Appendix C
Encapsulating Primitives _____ 211

Series Foreword
The Net Objectives Lean-Agile Series

Alan Shalloway, CEO, Net Objectives

If you are like me, you will just skim this foreword for the series and move on, figuring there is nothing of substance here. You will miss something of value if you do.

I want you to consider with me a tale that most people know but don't often think about. That tale illustrates what is ailing this industry. And it sets the context for why we wrote the Net Objectives Product Development Series and this particular book.

I have been doing software development since 1970. To me, it is just as fresh today as it was four decades ago. It is a never-ending source of fascination to me to contemplate how to do something better, and it is a never-ending source of humility to confront how limited my abilities truly are. I love it.

Throughout my career, I have also been interested in other industries, especially engineering and construction. Now, engineering and construction have suffered some spectacular failures: the Leaning Tower of Pisa, the Tacoma Narrows Bridge, the Hubble telescope. In its infancy, engineers knew little about the forces at work around them. Mostly, engineers tried to improve practices and to learn what they could from failures. It took a long time—centuries—before they acquired a solid understanding about how to do things.

No one would build a bridge today without taking into account long-established bridge-building practices (factoring in stress, compression, and the like), but software developers get away with writing code based on "what they like" every day, with little or no complaint from their peers. And developers are not alone: Managers often require people to work in ways that they know are counterproductive. Why do we work this way?

But this is only part of the story. Ironically, much of the rest is related to why we call this the Net Objectives Product Development Series. The Net Objectives part is pretty obvious. All of the books in this series were written either by Net Objectives staff or by those whose views are consistent with ours. Why product development? Because when building software, it is always important to remember that software development is really product development.

By itself, software has little inherent value. Its value comes when it enables delivery of products and services. Therefore, it is more useful to think of software development as part of product development—the set of activities we use to discover and create products that meet the needs of customers while advancing the strategic goals of the company.

Mary and Tom Poppendieck, in their excellent book *Implementing Lean Software Development: From Concept to Cash* (Addison-Wesley, 2006), note the following:

> *It is the product, the activity, the process in which software is embedded that is the real product under development. The software development is just a subset of the overall product development process. So in a very real sense, we can call software development a subset of product development. And thus, if we want to understand lean software development, we would do well to discover what constitutes excellent product development.*

In other words, software in itself isn't important. It is the value that it contributes—to the business, to the consumer, to the user—that is important. When developing software, we must always remember to look to what value is being added by our work. At some level, we all know this. But so often organizational "silos" work against us, keeping us from working together, from focusing on efforts that create value.

The best—and perhaps only—way to achieve effective product development across an organization is a well-thought-out combination of principles and practices that relate both to our work and to the people doing it. These must address more than the development team, more than management, and even more than the executives driving everything. That is the motivation for the Net Objectives Product Development Series.

Too long, this industry has suffered from a seemingly endless swing of the pendulum from no process to too much process and then back to no process: from heavyweight methods focused on enterprise control to disciplined teams focused on the project at hand. The time has come for management and individuals to work together to maximize the production of business value across the enterprise. We believe lean principles can guide us in this.

Lean principles tell us to look at the systems in which we work and then relentlessly improve them in order to increase our speed and quality (which will drive down our cost). This requires the following:

- Business to select the areas of software development that will return the greatest value

- Teams to own their systems and continuously improve them

- Management to train and support their teams to do this

- An appreciation for what constitutes quality work

It may seem that we are very far from achieving this in the software-development industry, but the potential is definitely there. Lean principles help with the first three, and understanding technical programming and design has matured far enough to help us with the fourth.

As we improve our existing analysis and coding approaches with the discipline, mind-set, skills, and focus on value that lean, agile, patterns, and Test-Driven Development teach us, we will help elevate software development from being merely a craft into a true profession. We have the knowledge required to do this; what we need is a new attitude.

The Net Objectives Lean-Agile Series aims to develop this attitude. Our goal is to help unite management and individuals in work efforts that "optimize the whole":

- **The whole organization.** Integrating enterprise, team, and individuals to work best together.

- **The whole product.** Not just its development but also its maintenance and integration.

- **The whole of time.** Not just now but in the future. We want sustainable ROI from our effort.

This Book's Role in the Series

Somewhere along the line, agile methods stopped including technical practices. Fortunately, they are coming back. Scrum has finally acknowledged that technical practices are necessary in order for agility to manifest itself well. Kanban and eXtreme Programming (XP) have become interesting bedfellows when it was observed that XP had one-piece flow ingrained in its technical practices.

This book was written as a stop-gap measure to assist teams that have just started to do lean, kanban, scrum, or agile. Regardless of the approach, at some point teams are going to have to code differently. This is a natural evolution. For years I have been encouraged that most people who take our training clearly know almost everything they need to know. They just need a few tweaks or a few key insights that will enable them to be more effective in whatever approach they will be using.

Why is this book a "stop-gap measure"? It's because it is a means to an end. It offers a minimal set of skills that developers need to help them on their way toward becoming adept at incremental development. Once developers master these skills, they can determine what steps they need to take next or what skills they need to acquire next. They are readied for an interesting journey. This book offers the necessary starting point.

The End of an Era, the Beginning of a New Era

I believe the software industry is at a crisis point. The industry is continually expanding and becoming a more important part of our everyday lives. But software development groups are facing dire problems. Decaying code is becoming more problematic. An overloaded workforce seems to have no end in sight. Although agile methods have brought great improvements to many teams, more is needed. By creating a true software profession, combined with the guidance of lean principles and incorporating agile practices, we believe we can help uncover the answers.

Since our first book appeared, I have seen the industry change considerably. The advent of kanban, in particular, has changed the way many teams and organizations do work. I am very encouraged.

I hope you find this book series to be a worthy guide.

—*Alan Shalloway*
CEO, Net Objectives
Achieving enterprise and team agility

Preface

Although this is a technical book, the idea of it sprang from the Net Objectives' agile development courses. As I was teaching teams how to do scrum or lean, students would often ask me, "How are we supposed to be able to build our software in stages?" The answer was readily apparent to me. What they were really asking was, "How can we best learn how to build our software in stages?" I knew of three approaches:

- **Read books.** I am confident that anyone who read and absorbed the books *Design Patterns Explained: A New Perspective on Object-Oriented Design* and *Emergent Design: The Evolutionary Nature of Professional Software Development* would know how to write software in stages.

- **Take courses.** This is a better approach. The combination of Net Objectives courses—Design Patterns and Emergent Design—can't be beat.

- **Learn about trim tabs.** The trim tabs of software development make building software in stages more efficient.

The first one requires a big investment in time. The second one requires a big investment in money. The third one requires less of both. Unfortunately, there is no place where these "trim tabs" are described succinctly.

What are trim tabs? They are structures on airplanes and ships that reduce the amount of energy needed to control the flaps on an airplane or the rudder of a ship. But what I mean comes from something Bucky Fuller once said.

Something hit me very hard once, thinking about what one little man could do.

Think of the Queen Mary—the whole ship goes by and then comes the rudder. And there's a tiny thing at the edge of the rudder called a trim tab.

It's a miniature rudder. Just moving the little trim tab builds a low pressure that pulls the rudder around. Takes almost no effort at all. So I said that the little individual can be a trim tab. Society thinks it's going right by you, that it's left you altogether. But if you're doing dynamic things mentally, the fact is that you can just put your foot out like that and the whole big ship of state is going to go.

So I said, call me Trim Tab.

In other words, these are the actions and insights that give the most understanding with the least investment. In our design patterns courses, we identify three essential trim tabs. Students who do these three things see tremendous improvements in their design and programming abilities. What were these three? Why, they are described in chapters in this book of course:

- Programming by intention
- Separate use from construction
- Consider testability before writing code

These three are very simple to do and take virtually no additional time over not doing them. All three of these are about encapsulation. The first and third encapsulate the implementation of behavior while the second focuses explicitly on encapsulating construction. This is a very important theme because encapsulation of implementation is a kind of abstraction. It reminds us that we are implementing "a way" of doing things—that there may be other ways in the future. I believe forgetting this is the main cause of serious problems in the integration of new code into an existing system.

A fourth trim tab that I recommend is to follow Shalloway's principle. This one takes more time but is always useful.

This book is a compilation of the trim tabs that Net Objectives' instructors and coaches have found to be essential for agile developers to follow to write quality code in an efficient manner. It is intended to be read in virtually any order and in easy time segments. That said, the chapters are sequenced in order to support the flow of ideas.

Acknowledgments

Note from Alan Shalloway

We are indebted to Buckminster Fuller in the writing of this book for many reasons. First, a little bit about Bucky, as he was affectionately known by his friends. I am sorry to say I never met him, but he certainly would have been a dear friend of mine if I had. Bucky was best known for the invention of the geodesic dome and the term "Spaceship Earth." He also coined the term "synergetics"—the study of systems in transformation—which is essentially what we do at Net Objectives. Of course, most relevant is that his use of the term "trim tab" (discussed in the preface) was the actual inspiration for this book.

He was also an inspiration for me to always look for better ideas. This quote is my all-time favorite Buckyism:

> I am enthusiastic over humanity's extraordinary and sometimes very timely ingenuity. If you are in a shipwreck and all the boats are gone, a piano top buoyant enough to keep you afloat that comes along makes a fortuitous life preserver. But this is not to say that the best way to design a life preserver is in the form of a piano top. I think that we are clinging to a great many piano tops in accepting yesterday's fortuitous contrivings as constituting the only means for solving a given problem.

All these are good reasons, of course. But in truth, I realized I wanted to make a special acknowledgment for Bucky because he has been an inspiration in my life from, ironically, mostly the moment he passed away in 1983. He was not just one of these vastly intelligent men or one of these great humane folks. He was a rare, unique combination of both. If you are not familiar with this great man, or even if you are, I suggest you check out the Buckminster Fuller Institute (http://www .bfi.org).

We Also Want to Acknowledge

This book represents our view of those skills that we believe every agile software developer should possess. However, we did not come up with this guidance on our own, and we owe a debt of sincere gratitude to the following individuals.

Christopher Alexander, master architect and author of *The Timeless Way of Building*. Although he is not a technical expert, Alexander's powerful ideas permeate nearly all aspects of our work, most especially the concept "design by context."

Erich Gamma, Richard Helm, Ralph Johnson, and John Vlissides, authors of the seminal book *Design Patterns: Elements of Reusable Object-Oriented Software*. Although we hope to have significantly advanced the subject of their work, it was the genesis of much of the wisdom that guides us today.

James Coplien wrote the thesis "Multi-Paradigm Design" that became the book that taught us about Commonality-Variability Analysis. This in turn helped us understand how to use patterns and objects in a way that fits the problem domain before us. Jim's work is a powerful enabler of many of the skills we teach in this book.

Martin Fowler, author of *Refactoring* and *UML Distilled*, as well as many other thoughtful and incredibly useful books. Martin is definitely the developer's friend.

Ward Cunningham, one of the author/inventors of eXtreme Programming and the progenitor of the role of testing in the daily life of the software developer. Countless good things have come from that central idea. Also, Ward, thanks so much for inventing wikis.

Robert C. Martin, author of *Agile Software Development* and many other books and articles. "Uncle Bob" teaches how various critical coding skills work together to make software that is readable, scalable, maintainable, and elegant.

In addition to these individual authors and thought leaders, we also want to acknowledge the thousands of students and consulting clients who have contributed endlessly to our understanding of what good software is and how to make it. It has been said that the good teacher always learns from the student, and we have found this to be true to an even greater degree than we expected when Net Objectives was founded more than 10 years ago. Our clients have given us countless opportunities to expand our thinking, test our ideas, and gain critical feedback on their real-world application.

There would be no Net Objectives without our customers. We love our customers.

About the Authors

 **Alan Shalloway** is the founder and CEO of Net Objectives. With more than 40 years of experience, Alan is an industry thought leader in lean, kanban, product portfolio management, scrum, and agile design. He helps companies transition to lean and agile methods enterprisewide as well teaches courses in these areas. Alan has developed training and coaching methods for lean-agile that have helped Net Objectives' clients achieve long-term, sustainable productivity gains. He is a popular speaker at prestigious conferences worldwide. He is the primary author of *Design Patterns Explained: A New Perspective on Object-Oriented Design* and *Lean-Agile Pocket Guide for Scrum Teams*. Alan has worked in dozens of industries over his career. He is a cofounder and board member for the Lean Software and Systems Consortium. He has a master's degree in computer science from M.I.T. as well as a master's degree in mathematics from Emory University. You can follow Alan on Twitter @alshalloway.

 **Scott Bain** is a 35+-year veteran in computer technology, with a background in development, engineering, and design. He has also designed, delivered, and managed training programs for certification and end-user skills, both in traditional classrooms and via distance learning. Scott teaches courses and consults on agile analysis and design patterns, advanced software design, and sustainable Test-Driven Development. Scott is a frequent speaker at developer conferences such as JavaOne and SDWest. He is the author of *Emergent Design: The Evolutionary Nature of Professional Software*

Development, which won a Jolt Productivity Award and is now available from Addison-Wesley.

Ken Pugh is a fellow consultant with Net Objectives. He helps companies transform into lean-agility through training and coaching. His particular interests are in communication (particularly effectively communicating requirements), delivering business value, and using lean principles to deliver high quality quickly. He also trains, mentors, and testifies on technology topics ranging from object-oriented design to Linux/Unix. He has written several programming books, including the 2006 Jolt Award winner, *Prefactoring: Extreme Abstraction, Extreme Separation, Extreme Readability*. His latest book is *Lean-Agile Acceptance Test Driven Development: Better Software Through Collaboration*. He has helped clients from London to Boston to Sydney to Beijing to Hyderabad. When not computing, he enjoys snowboarding, windsurfing, biking, and hiking the Appalachian Trail.

Amir Kolsky is a senior consultant, coach, and trainer for Net Objectives. Amir has been in the computer sciences field for more than 25 years. He worked for 10 years in IBM Research and spent 9 more years doing chief architect and CTO work in assorted companies big and small. He has been involved with agile since 2000. He founded MobileSpear and subsequently XPand Software, which does agile coaching, software education, and agile projects in Israel and Europe. Amir brings his expertise to Net Objectives as a coach and trainer in lean and agile software processes, tools, and practices, Scrum, XP, design patterns, and TDD.

PART I

The Core Trim Tabs

CHAPTER 1

Programming by Intention

*Everything old is new again. The folks who brought us the eXtreme Program-
ming (XP) books[1] were, among other things, promoting a set of best practices
in software development. One of them, which they termed "Programming by
Intention," was not actually new but was something that had been a very common coding technique in languages like COBOL and Smalltalk (usually called
"top-down" programming) years before. That's actually a good thing; time-tested
practices are often the most credible ones, because they've proven their value over
and over again in realistic circumstances. In this chapter, we'll examine this practice, first by simply demonstrating it and then by investigating the advantages we
gain by following it. Finally, we'll discuss it as it relates to testing and testability
and to design.*

Programming by Intention: A Demonstration

You need to write some code. What you need to create is just a service
that takes a business transaction and commits it. You've decided (rightly
or wrongly) to simply create a single object, with a simple public method
that does the work.

The requirements are the following:

- The transaction will begin as a standard ASCII string.

- The string must be converted to an array of strings, which are
  tokens in the domain language being used for the transaction.

---

1. These include Kent Beck, Cynthia Andres, Martin Fowler, James Newkirk, Robert
   Martin, Ron Jeffries, Lisa Crispin, Tip House, Ann Anderson, and Chet Hendrickson.

- Each token must be normalized (first character uppercase, all others lowercase, spaces and nonalphanumeric characters removed).

- Transactions of more than 150 tokens should be committed differently (using a different algorithm) than smaller transactions, for efficiency.

- The API method should return a true if the commit succeeds and should return a false if it fails.

We're leaving out some details—such as what the commitment algorithms actually are—to focus narrowly on the practice we're interested in here.

In learning to write in a programming language, you train your mind to break down problems into functional steps. The more code you write, the better your mind gets at this sort of problem solving. Let's capitalize on that.

As you think about the previous problem, each bullet point represents one of these functional steps. In writing your code, you will have the *intention* of solving each one as you go. Programming by Intention says, rather than actually writing the code in each case, instead *pretend* that you already have an ideal method, local in scope to your current object, that does precisely what you want. Ask yourself, "What parameters would such an ideal method take, and what would it return? And, what name would make the most sense to me, right now, as I imagine this method already exists?"

Now, since the method does not actually exist, you are not constrained by anything other than your intentions (hence, you are "programming by" them). You would tend to write something like this:

```
public class Transaction {
  public Boolean commit(String command) {
    Boolean result = true;
    String[] tokens = tokenize(command);
    normalizeTokens(tokens);
    if(isALargeTransaction(tokens)) {
      result = processLargeTransaction(tokens);
    } else {
      result = processSmallTransaction(tokens);
    }
    return result;
  }
}
```

The commit() method is the defined API of our object. It's public, of course, so that it can serve up this behavior to client objects. All of these other methods (tokenize(), isALargeTransaction(), process-LargeTransaction(), and processSmallTransaction()) are not part of the API of the object but are simply the functional steps along the way. They are often called "helper methods" as a result. For now, we'll think of them as private methods (however, as we'll see, that's not always literally true). The point is that their existence is part of the internal implementation of this service, not part of the way it is used from the outside.

And, they don't really exist yet. If you try to compile your code, naturally the compiler will report that they do not exist (we like that, though...it's a sort of to-do list for the next steps). They have to be created for the code to compile, which is what we must do next.[2]

In writing this way, we allow ourselves to focus purely on how we're breaking down the problem and other issues of the overall context we're in. For instance, we have to consider whether the String array being used is, in our implementation language, passed by reference or passed by copy (obviously we're imagining a language where they are passed by reference; otherwise, we'd be taking tokens back as a return). What we don't think about, at this point, are implementation details of the individual steps.

So, what's the point? There are actually many advantages gained here, which we'll investigate shortly, but before we do that, let's acknowledge one important thing: This is not hard to do. This is not adding more work to our plate. The code we write is essentially the same that we would have written if we'd simply written all the code into one big method (like our "programs" back in the day, one big stream of code logic). We're simply writing things in a slightly different way and in a slightly different order.

That's important. Good practices should, ideally, be things you can do all the time and can promote across the team as something that should always be done. This is possible only if they are very low cost—essentially free—to do.

---

2. Or someone else will. Sometimes breaking a problem up like this allows you to hand out tasks to experts. Perhaps someone on your team is an expert in the domain language of the tokens; you might hand off the tokenize() and normalize() methods to them.

Advantages

So again, what's the point of programming in this way?

Something so terribly simple actually yields a surprising number of beneficial results while asking very little, almost nothing, of you in return. We'll summarize these benefits in a list here and then focus on each individually.

If you program by intention, your code will be

- More cohesive (single-minded)
- More readable and expressive
- Easier to debug
- Easier to refactor/enhance, so you can design it minimally for now
- Easier to unit test

And, as a result of these benefits there are others: Your code will be easier to modify/extend. The additional benefits include the following:

- Certain patterns will be easier to "see" in your code.
- You will tend to create methods that are easier to move from one class to another.
- Your code will be easier to maintain.

Method Cohesion

One of the qualities of code that tends to make it easier to understand, scale, and modify is cohesion. Basically, we like software entities to have a single-minded quality, in other words, to have a single purpose or reason for existing.

Let's take classes, for instance. A class should be defined by its responsibility, and there should be only one general responsibility per class. Within a class are methods, state, and relationships to other objects that enable the class to fulfill its responsibility. Class cohesion is strong when all the internal aspects of a class relate to each other within the context of the class's single responsibility.

You might argue in our earlier example that some of the things we're doing are actually separate responsibilities and should be in other classes. Perhaps; this is a tricky thing to get right.[3] However, even if we

---

3. ...which is not to say we don't have some help for you on class cohesion. See Chapter 3, Define Tests Up Front, for more on this.

don't always get that right, we can get another kind of cohesion right at least most of the time if we program by intention.

Method cohesion is also an issue of singleness, but the focus is on function. We say a method is strongly cohesive if the method accomplishes one single functional aspect of an overall responsibility.

The human mind is pretty single-threaded. When people "multitask," the truth is usually that they are actually switching quickly between tasks; we tend to think about one thing at a time. Programming by Intention capitalizes on this fact, allowing the singleness of your train of thought to produce methods that have this same singleness to them.

This cohesion of methods is a big reason that we get many of the other benefits of Programming by Intention.

Readability and Expressiveness

Looking back at our initial code example, note how readable it is.

```
public class Transaction {
  public Boolean commit(String command) {
    Boolean result = true;
    String[] tokens = tokenize(command);
    normalizeTokens(tokens);
    if(isALargeTransaction(tokens)) {
      result = processLargeTransaction(tokens);
    } else {
      result = processSmallTransaction(tokens);
    }
    return result;
  }
}
```

The code essentially "says" the following: "We are given a command to commit. We tokenize the command, normalize the tokens, and then, depending on whether we have a large set of tokens or not, we process them using either the large transaction mechanism or the small one. We then return the result."

Because we are not including the "how" in each case, only the "what," we can examine the process with a quick read of the method and easily understand how this all works. Sometimes, that's all we want—to quickly understand how something works.

This lends readability, but it is also expressive. Note that we did not include any comments in this code, and yet it's still easy to "get." That's because those things that we would have included in comments are now instead the actual names of the methods.

Comments are expressive, too, but the problem with them is that they are ignored by the compiler[4] and often by other programmers who don't trust them to be accurate. A comment that has been in the code for a long time is unreliable, because we know that the code may have been changed since it was written, and yet the comment may not have been updated. If we trust the comment, it may mislead us, and there is no way to know one way or the other. We are forced to investigate the code, and so the expressiveness evaporates. Hence, comments may be ignored by programmers as well, making them less than useful.[5]

The central, organizing method in Programming by Intention contains all the steps but very little or no actual implementation. In a sense, this is another form of cohesion: The process by which something is done is separated from the actual accomplishing of that thing.

Another thing that tends to make code both readable and expressive is that the names of the entities we create should express the intention we had in creating them. When methods are cohesive, it is easy to name them with a word or two that comprehensively describes what they do, without using lots of underscores and "ands" and "ors" in the names. Also, since we name the methods before they actually exist, we tend to pick names that express our thinking. We call names of this type "intention-revealing names" because they disclose the intention of the name. We want to avoid picking names that make sense after you understand what the function does but can be easily misinterpreted before its intention is explained by someone who knows what is going on.

Comments as a Code Smell

Although we're not claiming that you shouldn't write comments, certain comments are actually a type of code smell. For example, let's say you had written something like the following:

```
public class Transaction {
  public Boolean commit(String command){
    Boolean result = true;
    Some code here
    Some more code here
```

---

4. Not all comments are to be avoided, however. If the comment exists to make the code more readable, change the code to make it more readable on its own. If the comment exists to explain the purpose of a class or method or to express a business issue that drives the code, these can be very helpful to have.
5. They are less than useful because sometimes someone believes them when they are wrong.

```
    Even some more code here that sets tokens
    Some code here that normalizes Tokens
    Some more code here that normalizes Tokens
    Even more code here that normalizes Tokens
    Code that determines if you have a large transaction
    Set lt= true if you do
    if (lt) {
      Some code here to process large transactions
      More code here to process large transactions
    } else {
      Some code here to process small transactions
      More code here to process small transactions
    }
    return result;
  }
}
```

You might look at this and say, "Wow, I don't understand it; let's add some comments," and you'd create something like the following:

```
public class Transaction {
  public Boolean commit(String command){
    Boolean result = true;

    // tokenize the string
    Some code here
    Some more code here
    Even some more code here that sets tokens

    // normalize the tokens
    Some code here that normalizes Tokens
    Some more code here that normalizes Tokens
    Even more code here that normalizes Tokens

    // see if you have a large transaction
    Code that determines if you have a large transaction
    Set lt= true if you do
    if (lt) {
      // process large transaction
      Some code here to process large transactions
      More code here to process large transactions
    } else {
      // process small transaction
      Some code here to process small transactions
      More code here to process small transactions
    }
    return result;
  }
}
```

Note that you've inserted comments that describe what is going on after writing the code. These comments would not be needed if we had programmed by intention. The methods we've used in place of the comments are more useful because they *have* to be up-to-date in order to compile.

Debugging

In most of the courses we teach at Net Objectives, somewhere along the way we'll ask people if they think they spend a lot of time fixing bugs. Unless they have already been a student of ours, they'll tend to say yes, that's a significant part of what makes software development tricky.[6]

We point out, however, that debugging really consists largely of *finding* the bugs in a system, whereas fixing them once they are located is usually less problematic. Most people agree to that almost immediately.

So, the real trick in making code that you will be able to debug in the future is to do whatever you can to make bugs easy to find. Naturally, you should try to be careful to avoid writing them in the first place, but you can be only so perfect, and you're probably not the only person who'll ever work on this code.

When you program by intention, the tendency is to produce methods that do one thing. So, if something in your system is not working, you can do the following:

1. Read the overall method to see how everything works.

2. Examine the details of the helper method that does the part that's not working.

That's almost certainly going to get you to the bug more quickly than if you have to wade through a big blob of code, especially if it contains many different, unrelated aspects of the system.

Legacy systems, for example, are tough to debug, and there are many reasons for this. One big one, however, is that often they were written in a monolithic way, so you end up printing the code, breaking out the colored highlighters, and marking code blocks by what they do. "I'll mark the database stuff in yellow, the business rules in blue, ..." It's laborious, error-prone, boring, and not a good use of a developer's time.

Let the computer do the grunt work.

---

6. If they are students of ours, they've heard this question from us before; we're not claiming our students don't write bugs.

Refactoring and Enhancing

It's hard to know exactly how far to go in design and how much complexity to add to a system in your initial cut at creating it. Because complexity is one of the things that can make a system hard to change, we'd like to be able to design minimally, adding only what is really needed to make the system work.

However, if we do that, we're likely to get it wrong from time to time and fail to put in functionality that is actually needed. Or, even if we get it right, the requirements of our customers, our stakeholders, or the marketplace can change the rules on us after the system is up and running.

Because of this, we often have to do the following:

- Refactor the system (changing its structure while preserving its behavior)

- Enhance the system (adding or changing the behavior to meet a new need)

Refactoring is usually thought of as "cleaning up" code that was poorly written in the first place. Sometimes it is code that has decayed because of sloppy maintenance or changes made under the gun without enough regard to code quality. Refactoring can also be used to improve code once it is clear it should have been designed differently after more is known about the program.

Martin Fowler wrote a wonderful book in 1999 called *Refactoring*[7] that codified the various ways in which these kinds of behavior-preserving changes can be made and gave each way a name (often called a "move").

One of the refactoring moves that most people learn first when studying this discipline is called Extract Method; it takes a piece of code out of the middle of a large method and makes it into a method of its own, calling this new method from the location where the code used to be. Because temporary method variables also have to move, and so forth, a number of steps are involved.

Many of the other refactoring moves in the book begin by essentially stating "Before you can do this, you must do Extract Method over and over until all of your methods are cohesive." However, you'll find if you program by intention, you've already done this part. In his

---

7. Fowler, Martin, et al. *Refactoring: Improving the Design of Existing Code*. Reading, MA: Addison-Wesley, 1999.

book *Prefactoring*,[8] Ken Pugh examines extensively how simple, sensible things like Programming by Intention can help you.

If you know that your code has routinely been "prefactored" in this way, your expectation about how difficult it will be to refactor it in other ways will be ameliorated, because code that already has method cohesion is simply easier to refactor.

Similarly, Programming by Intention can make it easier to enhance your system. Let's go back to our transaction processing example.

Imagine that six months after this code was put into production, a new requirement is added to the mix: Because of the way some third-party applications interact with the transaction processing, we have to convert some tokens (there's a list of a dozen or so) from an older version to the one supported by our system. The notion of "updating" all the tokens is now something we must always perform in case the command string contains deprecated tokens from the domain language.

The change here would be reasonably trivial and could be made with a high degree of confidence.

```
public class Transaction {
  public Boolean commit(String command){
    Boolean result = true;
    String[] tokens = tokenize(command);
    normalizeTokens(tokens);
    updateTokens(tokens);
    if(isALargeTransaction(tokens)){
      result = processLargeTransaction(tokens);
    } else {
      result = processSmallTransaction(tokens);
    }
    return result;
  }
}
```

The next step would be to write the updateTokens() method, but in so doing we note that the likelihood of doing any damage to the code in the rest of the system is extremely low. In fact, making changes to any of the helper methods can be done with a fair degree of confidence that we are changing only what we intend. Cohesion tends to lead to encapsulation[9] like this.

---

8. Pugh, Ken. *Prefactoring*. Cambridge, MA: O'Reilly, 2005.
9. See Chapter 5, Encapsulate That!, for more information on this.

Unit Testing

In Programming by Intention, we're not trying to broaden the interface of the object in question; rather, we're ensuring that we're defining the interface prior to implementing the code within it. In fact, we want to follow the general advice on design that patterns promote insofar as we'd like the clients that use our service to be designed purely to its interface, not to any implementation details.

So, at least initially, we'd like to keep all these "helper methods" hidden away, because they are not part of the API of the service and we don't want any other object, now or in the future, to become coupled to them (the way they work or even that they exist at all). We'd like to be able to change our mind in the future about the exact way we're breaking up this problem and not have to make changes elsewhere in the system where this object is used.

However, it would seem to work *against* testing this object, if we make all the helper methods private (see Figure 1.1).

Private methods cannot be called by the unit test either, so the only test we can write is of the `commit()` method, which means we have to test the entire behavior in a single test. Such a test may be more complex than we want, and also we'll be writing a test that could fail for a number of different reasons, which is not what we'd prefer.[10]

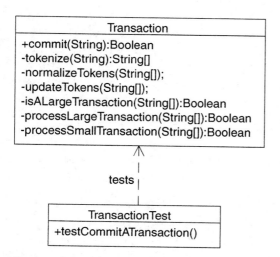

Figure 1.1   Programming by Intention, private methods

---

10. See Chapter 3, Define Tests Up Front, for more information on this issue.

If we can solve this conundrum, however, note that separating the different aspects of this overall behavior into individual methods makes them, at least in theory, individually testable, because they are not coupled to one another. Much as the client of this class is coupled only to its interface, the API method is coupled to the helper methods only though their interfaces.

So, how do we deal with the untestability of private methods? There are three general possibilities.

- We don't test them individually, but only through the commit() method. In unit testing, we want to test *behavior*, not *implementation*, so if these helper methods are really just steps in a single behavior, we don't want to test them. We want to be able to refactor them (even eliminate them) and have the same tests pass as before we refactored.

- We need to test them individually, as a practical matter. Even though they are "just the steps," we know there are vulnerabilities that make them somewhat likely to fail at some point. For efficiency and security, we want to be able to test them separately from the way they are used. In this case, we need to get a little clever and use testing tricks. These can be very language-dependent but include the following: making the test a "friend" of the class (in C++), wrapping the private method in a delegate and handing the delegate to the test, also known as a "testing proxy" (in .NET), making the methods protected and deriving the test from the class, and so on. Beware of overusing these tricks, however; not all developers will readily understand what you have done, they often don't port well from one language/platform to another, and we don't want to couple our tests tightly to implementation unnecessarily.

- Maybe these helper methods are not merely "steps along the way" but are, in fact, different behaviors that deserve their own tests. Maybe they are *used* in this class, but they are, in implementation, entirely separate responsibilities. Note that the desire to test this class is forcing us to look at this "Are they really just steps?" issue, which is an important aspect of design. If this is the case, then we need to revisit our design. For example, let's say we determine that the step that normalizes the tokens is really something that legitimately should be tested on its own. We could change the design just enough (see Figure 1.2).

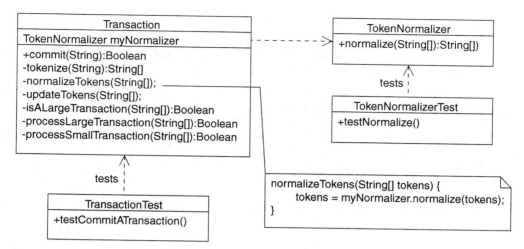

Figure 1.2   Design change

You'll note that the *use* of `TokenNormalizer` is private. Nothing outside `Transaction` is coupled to the fact that `TokenNormalizer` is used there.[11] However, the *implementation* of `TokenNormalizer` is accessible through its own API and is thus testable on its own.

Also, you'll note that because the normalization code was in a method by itself in the first place, it is pretty easy to pull it out now into its own class. Extracting a class is usually fairly trivial if methods are cohesive from the get-go. We're making this decision just as we need it, based on the realization that the desire to test is providing us.

Another reason we might have seen this would be if another entity in the system also had to perform token normalization. If the algorithm is stuck in a private method in `Transaction`, it's not usable in another context, but if it is in a class by itself, it is. Here the desire to avoid code duplication[12] is leading us to this same just-in-time decision.

Easier to Modify/Extend

Given the previous improvements to the quality of the code as a result of Programming by Intention, it should be evident that modifying and extending your code should be easier to do. We know from experience

---

11. This does raise the question, "How does Transaction obtain an instance of `TokenNormalizer`?" See Chapter 2, Separate Use from Construction, for a discussion on this issue.
12. See Chapter 4, Shalloway's Law and Shalloway's Principle, for a more thorough discussion on this concept.

that we will need to modify our code. It's also known from our experience that we don't know exactly what these modifications will be. Programming by Intention gives us a way to set up our code for modification while paying virtually no price for doing so.

Seeing Patterns in Your Code

We do a lot of design patterns training at Net Objectives, and we routinely write and speak about them at conferences. Invariably, once we are seen to be "pattern guys," someone will say, "The patterns are cool, but how do you know which one to use in a given circumstance?"

The answer to this question leads to a very long and (we think) interesting conversation, but sometimes you can see the pattern in your implementing code if you program by intention.

Let's alter our example slightly.

Let's say there are two completely different transaction types that go through the same steps (tokenize, normalize, update, process), but they implement all these steps differently, not just the processing step. If you programmed each of them by intention, although their implementing "helper" methods would all be different, the commit() method would look essentially the same. This would make the Template Method Pattern[13] sort of stand up and wave its hands at you (see Figure 1.3).

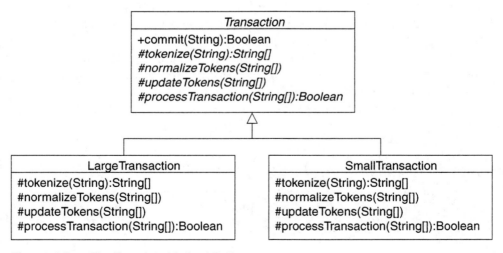

Figure 1.3   The Template Method Pattern

---

13. If you don't know the Template Method, pay a visit to www.netobjectivesrepository.com/
TheTemplateMethodPattern.

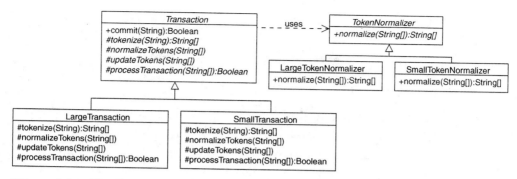

Figure 1.4   The Template Method and Strategy Patterns

Taking it a bit further and going back to the testability issue, we might start pulling one or more of these behaviors out, to make them testable, and in so doing discover opportunities for the Strategy Pattern. As before, we'll pull out normalization (see Figure 1.4).

Movable Methods

As we pointed out, the cohesion of a class is related to the notion that a class should, ideally, have a single responsibility. It may require many methods, member variables, and relationships to other objects to fulfill that responsibility, but there should be only one reason it exists or would have to be changed.[14]

Programming by Intention helps you create cohesive methods, through the simple expedient of creating those methods based on your own ability to do functional decomposition, but it does not, directly, do very much about class cohesion. Indeed, you could easily suggest that our `Transaction` class, as we initially coded it, was not very cohesive.

One way to improve class cohesion is to move methods and other members that it really should not have to other classes, perhaps new classes, and thus focus the class more narrowly. So, although Programming by Intention does not address class cohesion directly, it makes it easier for the developer to do so, through refactoring, as cohesion issues arise.

Why?

One reason is something we've already seen; Programming by Intention produces methods that have a single function. It's easier to move

---

14. This is also often called the Single Responsibility principle.

such a method because it avoids the problem of moving a method that contains some aspects that should not move. If a method does one thing, then if part of it needs to move, all of it needs to move.

However, there is another reason as well. Sometimes a method is hard to move because it directly relates to the state members that exist on the class. In moving the method, we have to move the state as well or find some way of making it available to the method in its new home, which can sometimes create an odd and confusing coupling.

We have noted that when we program by intention, we tend to pass the method whatever it is we want it to use and take the result as a return, rather than having the method work directly on the object's state. These methods move more easily because they are not coupled to the object they are in.

Going back to our example, we could have done the following:

```
public class Transaction {
  private String[] tokens;
  public Boolean commit(String command){
    Boolean result = true;
    tokenize(command);
    normalizeTokens();
    if(isALargeTransaction()){
      result = processLargeTransaction();
    } else {
      result = processSmallTransaction();
    }
      return result;
  }
}
```

We have made the token array a member of the class, and all the methods that used to take it as a parameter will now simply refer to it directly. There is nothing in Programming by Intention that *forces you* not to do this (any more than it forces you to refrain from naming your methods m1() and go()), but it's a more natural fit to your mind to pass parameters and take returns, and we have noticed this strong tendency in developers who adopt the practice.

Summary

One of the critical aspects of bringing any complex human activity to maturity is the discovery of important practices that improve the success of those engaged in it. Such practices should ideally do the following:

- Deliver a lot of value
- Be relatively easy to do
- Be relatively easy to promote and teach others to do
- Be low risk
- Be universal (you should not have to decide whether to follow them, in each given circumstance)

Programming by Intention is just such a practice. Give it a try! For most people, it takes only a few hours to realize that it's easy, it's fun, and it makes their code better without extra work.

CHAPTER 2

Separate Use from Construction

Moving from a procedural approach to an object-oriented one, with all its assumed benefits, tends to add an additional issue: instantiation. Whereas a procedural program or script tends to load, run, and then unload, the creation of object instances can be much more involved and can continue throughout the runtime life cycle of the software. Given this, developers often feel that solving "the instantiation" problem is job one. It is decidedly not. Also, typically instances will be created by the same code that uses them, often proximate to their use. This would seem to make the code more readable and easier to work with, but it often has a negative effect.

We will examine these issues, among others, that arise when we fail to separate the use of an instance from its construction.

An Important Question to Ask

In our technical classes, we usually ask the question, "When working on a system that is one to two years old and you need to add a new function, there is effort to write the function and then effort to integrate it into the system. Where do you spend most of your time? Writing the function or integrating it in?" About 95 percent of the time, the answer is "integrating it in."[1]

In our classes, we typically speculate that the integration process looks like this: "In my code that is using the new functionality, I have to go through it and see, ah, do I have this case? Yes, then I do this; else,

---

1. We base this on the answers we've gotten from our students over the past several years. Unfortunately, this ratio does not seem to be improving. The main exceptions to this are when the developers are properly using design patterns, when a complete set of automated unit tests is present, and when the function being written is amazingly complex.

I do that. Now here, I have to remember in this case I have this data to use, but in that case, this data means something else." Most of the people in the audience are nodding their heads in woeful agreement. A key problem with this approach is that adding features to your system requires you to change your client code to manage these features, all the while making the code more complex. Although it may not be a problem at the start, it can quickly decay into one.

If this seems familiar, you may have come to feel this is inevitable. You may have even been taught that this is an example of "entropy" and that there's really nothing you can do about it.

You may also notice that the cause of this is that while writing/ changing/managing client code, you have to be paying attention to the specific, concrete types of the objects you're dealing with. One promise of object-orientated programming is that we shouldn't necessarily have to be referring to objects by type, except in an abstract sense. In other words, we want to hide (encapsulate) the implementing object we are using at any given point in time.

People know that hiding implementation is important; it enables us to change implementations without changing the client code. But if you take a moment to reflect on this, you might realize that it is equally valuable to hide type as well. In other words, if you have two objects that conceptually do the same thing but whose type is exposed when they are used, then the client code couples to those particular objects when it should not. If we can hide the objects' concrete types, we'll make the calling code simpler and the system more maintainable.

Perspectives

A very simple, common bit of code that tends to appear throughout a system looks something like the following:

```
public class BusinessObject {
  public void actionMethod() {
    // Other things
    Service myServiceObject = new Service();
    myServiceObject.doService();
    // Other things
  }
}
```

There's nothing too surprising here. The `BusinessObject` class uses an instance of `Service` for part of its implementation. Perhaps it is a

Service object that is needed in several places in the system, and so it is implemented in an object. BusinessObject builds an instance of Service and then delegates to it for the needed behavior.

As natural and simple as this may seem, it is a mistake to be avoided. It creates two different relationships between the BusinessObject class and the Service class. BusinessObject is the creator of Service, but it is also the user of Service. There are significant advantages to be found in breaking these relationships apart.

Perspective of Creation

When one object creates an instance of another in languages like Java and C#, it by necessity must use the new keyword to do it. In modern languages, especially those that have automatic garbage collection, new is usually not something you can override. In other words, when the code in one object contains new Widget(), the object that is created as a result is precisely that, an instance of Widget, and no other class.

Also, in order for new Widget() to be a legal statement, Widget must be a concrete type, in other words, not an abstract class or interface. This means that any entity A that instantiates any other entity B using the new keyword directly is coupled to

- The actual type that is being instantiated

- The fact that the type is concrete

We say "coupled" because if either of these things were to change, then the entity doing the creation would have to be altered as well. Going back to our code example, if the class Service were to be changed to an interface, with a single implementing class called Service_Impl, then our code would no longer compile until we changed it to the following (the change is in bold, italic type).

```
public class BusinessObject {
  public void actionMethod() {
    // Other things
    Service myServiceObject = new Service_Impl();
    myServiceObject.doService();
    // Other things
  }
}
```

Note, also, that we get little or no value from upcasting the reference of `Service_Impl` to `Service`; since the code mentions the class `Service_Impl` anyway, the coupling is unavoidable. Let's contrast this with the perspective that one object has when it *uses* another object.

Perspective of Use

Let's alter our code example slightly. Rather than having `Business-Object` build its instance directly, we'll hand it one via its constructor.

You're probably thinking, "But wait, *something* had to create it." Yes, but for our purposes here, we'll leave that as an open issue for now and focus just on this class and its relationship to `Service` when we limit it to "use."

```
public class BusinessObject {
  private Service myServiceObject;
  public BusnessObject(Service aService) {
    myServiceObject = aService();
  }

  public void actionMethod() {
    // Other things
    myServiceObject.doService();
    // Other things
  }
}
```

If `Service` began as a concrete type and then later we changed it to an abstract type with a separate implementing class but no change was made to its interface (the `doService()` method), what would happen to this code? The answer is, nothing at all. Whatever implementing class was created, it would be implicitly upcast to `Service` and used as such.

If, on the other hand, we changed the method `doService()` in some way, say, changed its name or what parameters it takes, then this code would again fail to compile until we changed it to call the method in the altered way, whatever that might be.

In other words, if entity A calls methods on entity B but does not *create* entity B, then it is neither coupled to the specific concrete implementation that entity B happens to be nor to the fact that it is (or is not) a concrete type. Either of these things can changed without affecting entity A.

What You Hide You Can Change

Table 2.1 summarizes our points here.

Creators are coupled to type, while users are coupled to interface. Creators are coupled to what something is, while users are coupled to how something operates. These should be considered separate concerns, because they will often change for different reasons.

The problem with our initial code example is that `BusinessObject` establishes both of these perspectives relative to `Service`. It is the creator and the user of the `Service` and therefore is coupled to it very tightly. If `Service` changes in any way other than its internal implementation, `BusinessObject` will have to change as well.

The more we do this, the more work is required to alter an existing system, and the more likely we are to make mistakes.

"What you hide you can change" is a fairly common mantra among developers who favor encapsulated systems, but this really makes sense only when we define "can change" correctly. Otherwise, a developer reading such a statement might rightly think, "I can change anything I have the source code for."

When we say "can change," we really mean "can freely change": can change without having to be hesitant, without having to do extensive investigation of possible side effects, without stress and concern. Another way to say this is, "We can change it here, and we don't have to change it anywhere else."

Also, we must consider the likely motivations for change.

Why do interfaces change? Ideally, we'd like to create our interfaces from the point of view of those entities that consume their services, rather than from the point of view of any specific implantation code they contain. Thus, an interface will tend to change when the clients of that interface develop a new need.

Why do classes change from concrete to abstract? This usually happens when the design of the solution changes, arguably by adding some

Table 2.1   Coupling by Perspective

Perspective	Coupled to
Creation	The type being created and the fact that it is a concrete type
Use	The public method signature(s) being called

form of indirection in order to achieve polymorphism and/or to break a direct dependency for testing purposes or for reuse.

These are very different motivations and would tend to happen at different times in a product's development life cycle. Also, if we are circumspect about our interfaces, they will not change very frequently.[2] On the other hand, if we want to avoid overdesign in the early stages of development, we will frequently have to accommodate changing/adding/eliminating types later, without creating waste or risk.

Let's consider another approach.

```
public class BusinessObject {
  private Service myServiceObject;
    public BusnessObject() {
    myServiceObject = ServiceFactory.getService();
  }

  public void actionMethod() {
    // Other things
    myServiceObject.doService();
    // Other things
  }
}

class ServiceFactory{
  public static Service getService(){
  return new Service();
}
```

If the methods of `Service` change, this will affect the code in `BusinessObject` but not in `ServiceFactory` (they are not called by the factory). On the other hand, if the `Service` class itself changes, if it becomes an abstract class or interface, and if there may even be more than one implementing class, this will change `ServiceFactory` but not `BusinessObject`.

A design change is now possible, without changing `Business-Object` at all.

```
public class BusinessObject {
  private Service myServiceObject;
  public BusnessObject() {
    myServiceObject = ServiceFactory.getService();
  }
```

---

2. ...and even if they do, this likely can be accomplished using an Adapter or Façade Pattern; see our pattern repository at www.netobjectivesrepository.com if you are not familiar with these patterns.

```
  public void actionMethod() {
    // Other things
    myServiceObject.doService();
    // Other things
  }
}

class ServiceFactory{
  public static Service getService(){
    if (someCondition) {
      return new Service_Impl1();
    } else {
      return new Service_Impl2()
    }
  }
}

interface Service {
  void doService();
}

Service_Impl1 : Service {
  void doService() { // one implementation }
}

Service_Impl2 : Service
  void doService() { // different implementation }
}
```

What's the advantage? Are we simply not moving a problem from one place to another? Yes, but consider this: Today, software is becoming increasingly service-oriented (in fact, the term "Service-Oriented Architecture" represents a major movement in most large organizations). Thus, a service may develop many clients over time, creating economies of scale through reuse. In fact, you could reasonably say that the more clients a service serves, the more valuable it has proven itself to be.

However, it is far less common for us to create more than one factory for a given service. What we have done is moved our one and only change of existing code into a single, encapsulated place. Also, if the factory does nothing else except create instances, this will be a place with typically less complexity than other objects will tend to have.

Realistic Approach

The point here is that the entity that uses a service should not *also* create it, with the clear implication that "something else" will do so. What that something else is will vary.

In the previous example, we used a separate factory. Sometimes that is warranted. There are other ways.

- Objects can be created by a tool. Object-Relational mappers, store-retrieve persistence tools, and so on, separate the creation of the object(s) from their consumer(s).

- Objects can be created in one place, serialized, and then deserialized in another place by different entities. Again, the two operations are separated.

- Objects can be created outside the class and passed in via constructors or using setter() methods. This is often termed "dependency injection."

...and so on. The work required to use these methods is not always justified, however. If we are to do minimal designs, adding complexity only where it is actually warranted, we cannot decide to do any of these things with the anticipation that a class *may* change in the future. After all, anything could change.

Overdesign often comes from the desire to reduce risk in an environment where change is difficult to predict and where accommodating change by altering a design is perceived as dangerous and leading to decay. However, we want to reduce these concerns about change while adding the least complexity necessary.

What is needed is a bare-minimum practice that we can always engage in, when there is no justification for anything more complex. The following is what we[3] recommend.

```
public class BusinessObject {
  public void actionMethod() {
    // Other things
    Service myServiceObject = Service.getInstance();
    myServiceObject.doService();
    // Other things
  }
}

class Service {
  private Service(){
    //any needed construction behavior
  }
```

---

3. The origin of this idea is hard to determine, but we learned it here: Bloch, Joshua. *Effective Java Programming Language Guide.* Upper Saddle River, NJ: Prentice Hall, 2001.

```
  public static Service getInstance() {
    return new Service();
  }
  public void doService() {
    //implementation here
  }
}
```

We have added a few lines of code in `Service` and simply changed the new `Service()` that used to be in `BusinessObject` to `Service.getInstance()`.

This is simple and essentially no additional work, but it enables a clean transition to the following design, only when and if it ever becomes needed and even under that circumstance where many other clients besides `BusinessObject` are also using `Service` in this same way.

```
public class BusinessObject {
  public void actionMethod() {
    // Other things

    //No Change!
    Servicec myServiceObject = Service.getInstance();
    myServiceObject.doService();
    // Other things
  }
}

abstract class Service {
  private Service(){ //any needed construction behavior }
  public static Service getInstance() {
    return ServiceFactory.getService()
  }
  abstract void doService();
}

class ServiceFactory{
  public static Service getService(){
    if (someCondition) {
      return new Service_Impl1();
    } else {
      return new Service_Impl2()
    }
  }
}

Service_Impl1 : Service {
  void doService() { // one implementation }
}
```

```
Service_Impl2 : Service
  void doService() { // different implementation
}
```

Other Practical Considerations

In implementing this practice, or any practice, we have to keep pragmatic concerns in mind. Doctors always wash their hands, but they certainly would not refuse to give first aid to someone in an emergency without doing so. We always have to keep the real world in perspective when we apply a practice.

Here are some examples:

- We cannot always afford to make a constructor literally private. We have done so here in our examples to make it clear that new is not to appear in any of the client objects. If you remote objects, serialize them, and so on, you cannot make your constructors private and thus need to rely on the convention of using only get-Instance() in client objects as a best practice.

- Our factory uses a static method to build the object. We did this to keep the code brief and because we wanted to make a single, simple point. However, static methods are not recommended (except for getInstance()), and in practice we tend to make such factories singletons instead. See www.netobjectivesrepository.com/TheSingletonPattern for information on this pattern.

- Sometimes a separate factory is overkill for a simple conditional, and the object creation implementation can be left directly in the getInstance() method. However, this does weaken the object's cohesion.

- Sometimes the creation of the service object is a complex issue in and of itself. In this case, a separate factory is almost certainly warranted and may in fact be an implementation of a design pattern.

Timing Your Decisions

Even when we separate the use and construction issues, each is still a design consideration to be determined. We have to determine the proper objects and relationships for the desired behavior of the system and how to best get our instances created and "wired together." In each case, we are making design decisions that proceed from our analysis of the problem to be solved.

One question that often arises is, which decisions should we make first: our systemic design (for behavior) or how we will solve the instantiation problems.

It is very important that you hold off on committing to any particular instantiation scheme until you have a good idea of the design of your system. Determining your objects and their relationships must always come first, and not until you are fairly far along in making these determinations should the topic of object creation be addressed in any way.

Why? There are many different ways to solve the creational problems in object orientation; in fact, there are a number of well-established patterns, such as the Abstract Factory, Prototype, Singleton, Builder, and so forth. How do we pick the right one?

As in all pattern-oriented design, we must proceed from and be informed by the context of the problem we are solving, and in the case of instantiation, the objects and relationships in the design define this context. You cannot know which creational pattern is best before you know the nature of what is to be built.

Worse, if you do happen to select a pattern creation, perhaps capriciously ("I like Builders"), then almost certainly your system design will be whatever that creational pattern happens to build well and not the design that is uniquely appropriate to your problem domain.

Those of us who began as procedural programmers often have a hard time accepting this and adhering to it. We have a hard time resisting the instantiation issue, because it is an issue that did not really exist in the more straightforward load-and-run world of procedural programming.

Nevertheless, we need to be disciplined on this issue, and here is where colleagues can really help. In initial discussions about system design, we must always remind each other not to leap too quickly to instantiation/creation issues.

Using `getInstance()` in favor of the direct use of the constructor can help. Once this method is in place, it can delegate (in the future) to any sort of factory we might decide upon, with little or no change to the system.

Overloading and C++

If you are wondering what to do when you need to have overloaded constructors, the answer is simple: Create overloaded `getInstance` methods.

Those of you who are C++ programmers may notice the serious memory leaks here (if you are not a C++ programmer, please skip the rest of this paragraph). To solve this, you must add a corresponding static `releaseInstance()` method that you call where you would have called `delete` on the object. The `releaseInstance` object must take a pointer to the object being released, and it calls `delete` on the object. Note, however, that by shielding the creation and destruction of the objects, you may find you can get performance improvements by having the `getInstance()` and `releaseInstance()` methods control when things are constructed and deleted. For example, you can convert a regular object to a singleton without the using objects ever noticing (you'd change the `getInstance()` method to as needed for a singleton, and you'd have the `releaseInstance()` not do anything).

Validating This for Yourself

In our classes, we often pose the following situation and corresponding question to our students: "Imagine we divide this class so those on the left will decide what objects are needed and how they will be used. But, when using them, they don't have to worry about which particular objects they will use in a particular situation. Those people on the right side of the room will write factories that will give those people on the left the proper objects when asked for." That is, those on the left will have the perspective of use while those on the right will have the perspective of creation. "Which side of the room has the easier problem?"

Virtually everyone agrees that merely figuring out the rules for creation is much easier than figuring out which objects are needed, figuring out how to use them, and then implementing them. However, now consider how much work the side on the left has to do compared to what they would have to do without this division. It's almost certainly well less than half the work they had before. In other words, if you don't have to consider the particular objects you are using (the side on the right is doing that), your problem becomes significantly easier. Also, notice what happens when you get new functionality; you only have to write it and have the right side change the creating entities. Our biggest problem has just disappeared (integration of new code).

You should notice that this process—just considering the abstract type you have and not the specific implementation—encourages the thinking that "While I am implementing this now, I have other types that may be implemented later." This distinction between an implementation and the concept that it is an implementation of is very useful.

Summary

As consultants, we are often called in to help teams that are in trouble. In fact, if a team is "doing great," there would seem little reason to ask for help. Because of this, we see a lot of software systems that have significant challenges.

In your first day on-site as a consultant, you have to quickly find a way to make some kind of positive impact, but you are probably the least knowledgeable person about the system in question at that point, having just been introduced to it. To deliver value quickly, you need to know certain things to look for that a team in trouble will likely have failed to do.

One of the most common mistakes we see is the failure to separate the use of objects from their creation. This happens not because the development team is lazy or foolish. Most likely this is simply an issue they have not considered, and once they do, they can begin to introduce this practice and gain immense benefit from this single change.

There is a lesson in this. Value often flows from aligning ourselves with the essential nature, or truth, of something. The relationship "I use X" is very different from "I make X," and it is actually more natural to handle them in different places and in different ways.

I never make soup while bathing the baby or I'm likely to end up with onions in the shampoo.

CHAPTER 3

Define Tests Up Front

*With the advent of agile methods, Test-Driven Development (TDD) has been gaining momentum. A mantra of agile is that stories are **completed**, not merely written, every iteration. This means they have to go through testing to be considered "done, done, done." Many teams have experienced the productivity gains and value of TDD. Many teams have, unfortunately, shied away from it as well. We believe that the value and reason that TDD works are not fully appreciated. This chapter begins by defining testing and then discusses both why TDD works and why it isn't really testing up front.*

A Trim Tab: Testing and Testability

As mentioned in the preface, this book represents the set of trim tabs[1] we, at Net Objectives, consider to be most useful for enhancing the productivity of software developers. We consider the issue of testability (the focus of this chapter) to be, perhaps, the greatest of these. Hence, we could say this chapter is about the trim tabs of trim tabs.

What Is Testing?

Merriam Webster's dictionary defines test as "the procedure of submitting a statement to such conditions or operations as will lead to its proof or disproof or to its acceptance or rejection." This is testing as an action. However, a test can also be a noun, something that is "a basis of evaluation." We're sure you recollect a time someone put a "test" on your desk and then you had to take it. The test you were given in this case

---

1. If you haven't read the preface, please do so now, even if you understand what a trim tab is.

specified what you needed to know in order to get a good grade. The action of taking the test is something different altogether.

In the same way, tests in software are about what the software needs to do in order to be considered successfully implemented. This is why we can write tests before we have code to test. We are specifying what the software needs to do. We suggest this insight leads to the observation that test-first is really analysis-first using tests. In other words, we use the tests to determine the behavior we want of the functionality we are testing. This is a form of analysis.

But it is actually more than that; it is also a type of design using tests to accomplish the design. That is, simultaneously with the analysis, we are figuring out how to implement the interfaces of the functionality. We are splitting up the classes into their methods. We are, in essence, doing design.

Testability and Code Quality

Why is this useful? We suggest it's because testability is highly correlated to the code qualities we want to manifest, in particular, loose coupling, strong cohesion, and no redundancy. We can recollect times that at the start of testing our code we have remarked the following:

> "I can't test this code; it does too many things that are so intertwined." (weak cohesion)

> "I can't test this code without access to dozens of other things." (excessive coupling)

> "I can't test this code; it's been copied all over the place, and my tests will have to be duplicated over and over again." (redundancy)

> "I can't test this code; there are too many ways for external objects to change its internal state." (lack of encapsulation)

We've often summed it up by saying, "Gee, I wish they had thought of how this code was going to be tested while they were writing it!"

I'm (comment by Alan) kind of slow sometimes because it took me quite some time to realize the following:

> I should consider how my code is going to be tested before writing it!

The reason is clear: Testability is related to loose coupling, strong cohesion, no redundancy, and proper encapsulation. Another way to say this is that the tighter your coupling, the weaker your cohesion; the more your redundancy and the weaker your encapsulation, the harder it will be to test your code. Therefore, making your code easier to test will result in looser coupling, strong cohesion, less redundancy, and better encapsulation.

This leads to a new principle like the following:

> Considering how to test your code before you write it is a kind of design.

Since testability results in so many good code qualities and since it is done before you write your code, it is a very highly leveraged action. That is, a little work goes a long way; it's a great trim tab.

Case Study: Testability

Let's look at a case study. Let's say we have a piece of hardware whose status we need to detect (in other words, see whether it is functioning properly). After detecting the status, we need to send an encrypted message via TCP/IP to some monitoring device. If we were to ask you how to design the system, one of four choices probably comes to mind:

- Case 1: One class, one method that does it all (get status, encrypt, and transmit)
- Case 2: One class, four methods
  - ○ Control method that calls the other three methods that follow
  - ○ `getStatus()`
  - ○ `encrypt()`
  - ○ `transmit()`
- Case 3: Three classes, one or two methods in each
  - ○ `Hardware.getStatus()`
  - ○ `Encrypt.encrypt()`
  - ○ `Transmit.transmit()`
  - ○ `Hardware.getEncryptSendStatus()` calls the prior three methods
- Case 4: Four classes (a variant on the prior case where we have the control program in a separate class)

We can get into several "religious" conversations here as to which one is better. Note that the first one has poor cohesion and the likelihood of coupling the methods. If we start with that and need to modify the code (for example, use another encrypter), it may be difficult to do so.

Let's look at what happens if we design our code here with the simple mandate of making it as testable as possible. In this case, most people will select cases 2 to 4. Actually, most will pick 3 with a handful picking 2 or 4. Now, from a testability point of view, we would say 3 or 4 is the easiest. Why? What easier way of testing encryption is there than if it is in its own class? The same is true for the hardware and the transmitter. Some will say that as long as each function is in its own method and each method uses variables local to the method only, then it would be easy enough to extract the method when needed. It's kind of hard to win an argument for separate classes here if the person you are arguing with doesn't like lots of classes (or has misunderstood XP's mandate of fewest number of methods and classes). They can always say, "Look, the code is easy enough to see—why add the extra classes?"

This may not be a problem at this point. However, when methods like this are lumped together, we often take advantage of the fact that even private members are public to the classes' members. Hence, refactoring out the methods may or may not be easy. We also point out that you must instantiate the entire object, which may or may not be simple. For example, you may have to provide a valid TCP/IP connection to instantiate it. However, with the understanding that lumping all the methods together is acceptable only until one of the methods starts to vary (and then we'll have to pull it out), we wouldn't argue too long here. You should readily observe that considering the testability of the code here creates a better design.

By the way, it is worth noting that we are not suggesting that we have only one method per class. We are suggesting you have highly cohesive classes. In this example, each entity type didn't have a lot of functionality, so that's how things worked out.

Setting Ourselves Up for Change

You should note that the results we'll get with this approach will be code that is highly modularized, cohesive, and loosely coupled. This means we should be prepared for changes in the future. We'll take this a step further in Chapter 11, Refactor to the Open-Closed, which shows how design from test specifications such as we've done here sets the stage for extending our designs in an efficient manner.

Programmer as Frog

This brings up an interesting point. Why are programmers like frogs? In our classes we've gotten some pretty interesting answers to this question. They include we like finding bugs, we have warts, and you have to kiss a lot of programmers before you find your Prince Charming. But we're not looking for any of these answers.

It turns out, what we are referring to is actually an urban legend (we looked it up; we didn't try it, so don't report us to the ASPCA). It used to be believed that if you put a frog in hot water it'd immediately jump out. However, if you put it in a pot of room-temperature water and place the pot on the stove and heat it up, the frog will stay in the pot until it boiled to death. Now we know we would hop out of a pot that was on a stove (probably even before it got too hot!). So, why are we like frogs? It's because as developers we don't notice the slow degradation of our code.

We've all seen this in something we call "switch creep." The first switch we have isn't bad. The second one isn't bad either. But somewhere around the 57th switch, the water temperature is pretty up there!

This leads to a habit developers should get into: Don't degrade your code! Or, at least if you must, do it intentionally! That is, do it only when you know you are doing it. This takes discipline as well as team buy-in. But if you can do that, it also enables you to avoid slowly degrading your code.

We heard Ward Cunningham once say, "Spend as much time as you need to build the best-quality code you can, but don't add any functionality that you don't need right now."[2]

A Reflection on Up-Front Testing

As we were saying, up-front testing really isn't testing at all. It is really up-front design through the analysis of our tests. Can we take this testing even further? When XP came out and suggested doing unit tests, many of us realized that if we combined a series of unit tests together, we could get the equivalent of automated acceptance testing.

---

2. Said at an eXtreme Programming Seattle User Group meeting circa 2006.

However, there was a better way. With the invention of the Framework for Integrated Testing (FIT), defining acceptance tests became a separate process from combining unit tests. We now had an easy method to have nonprogrammers define and (virtually) implement acceptance tests. These two testing practices were still often practiced separately.

Eventually we came across Rick Mugridge's *FIT for Developing Software* (the first 50 pages of which are a must-read for all developers regardless of your testing practices). He eloquently states how defining acceptance tests up front improves the quality of the conversation between QAs, BAs, and devs. Given that these people will (or at least should) reflect on acceptance test definitions at some point, this implies we should pick the most beneficial time to do this—and that'd be *up front* (for a full exploration of this, please look at Chapter 7, Acceptance Test–Driven Development (ATDD)).

This creates value (better conversation, better understanding, clearer scope) without creating extra work. This leads to the insight that we should not drive our acceptance tests from our unit tests but rather do it the other way around since we need to be creating our acceptance tests first. In other words, our unit tests need to be created within the context of manifesting the behavior our acceptance tests dictate.

As a disciple of Christopher Alexander,[3] this makes sense in another way. Alexander's work proposes that designing from context (the big picture) creates better designs. However, we believe this is a broader principle than just a design principle. In general, we suggest that keeping in mind why you are doing something (the context) improves whatever it is you are doing (whether it is design or something else).

A big part of agile software development is discovering what the customer wants or needs. In doing this, one writes stories. Following Alexander's ideas here would mean that we should start with the big picture of the behavior we want and then go into the details. Again, this means driving unit tests within the context of the desired behavior. Hence, TDD is not even design-first as much as it is analysis and then design. So, perhaps we have Test Driven Analysis and Design and then Development (TDADD?).

But are we really testing first? We don't think so. Let's look at another activity: making and using plans. We can talk about planning in three ways.

---

3. Alexander, Christopher. *The Timeless Way of Building*. New York: Oxford University Press, 1979.

- Planning (the action of making the plan)
- Plan (a description of steps we intend to perform)
- Following the plan (doing these steps)

Now in testing, we have words for the second two steps but not for the first one. For example, the equivalent of a plan is a test specification. The equivalent of following the plan is running the tests. But what is the equivalent of planning? We would say it is creating the test specification. In other words, we have the following:

Plans	Tests
Planning	Creating the test specification
Plan	Test specification
Following the plan	Running the test

So, what we actually do is up-front Test Specification (OK, so we're being picky, but a test specification is different from running the test). Test specifications, of course, are another way of stating what the system needs to do; that is, it is analysis. We guess you could say we do TSDADD (Test-Specification Driven Analysis and Design and Development). No wonder they shortened it to TDD! Funny, however, that it wasn't given an intention-revealing name!

The challenge now with the term TDD is that it has a lot of latitude on what it means. Are we starting from the functional level (unit tests, TSDD)? Or the behavior of the system level (acceptance tests, TSDADD)? To avoid confusion in the rest of this chapter, we are going to refer to what we've been calling TSDADD (tongue-in-cheek) as Acceptance Test–Driven Development (or ATDD, which is described in detail in Chapter 7).[4] We will refer to the practice of writing unit tests first as UTDD. As stated earlier, starting from the behavioral level (the big picture) creates better conversations and context. Let's look at the advantages of doing so.

- Better design
- Improving the clarity of scope and avoiding excess work
- Reducing complexity

---

4. ATDD is very similar to Dan North's BDD but has some differences that we will not review here.

Better Design

Let's get back to Alexander's hypothesis. Alexander states that designing from context provides insights into what the functionality you are creating needs to do. Designing from the whole enables you to see how the smaller pieces should fit together. This is a fundamental design principle that works in other industries besides his (building construction). Although software development is not at all like building buildings, design patterns are somewhat based on this concept. One aspect of this is the Dependency Inversion principle. We should expect, then, that doing ATDD should result in better designs than the classic UTDD where we specified the pieces first and put them together.

Improving Clarity of Scope: Avoiding Excess Work

By providing our acceptance tests up front, we help the developer understand what is in the scope of the requirement. This prevents developers from overbuilding the system. This, of course, helps avoid excess work.

You might be concerned that this minimalistic design will not prepare us for future changes. But just the opposite is true. By having an automated test suite, high-quality code, and an understanding of quality design (design patterns), you set yourself up to be able to add design changes later, when you know they are needed and you know how to implement them. This is much more efficient than designing ahead of time.

Another way acceptance tests can help us avoid work is they can give us an indication of how far down we have to go in specifying unit tests. UTDD somewhat requires every function to be tested because the unit tests are your safety net. But in ATDD, the acceptance tests are your safety net; the unit tests are there to help you design your functions and to find errors faster (both good things but not always necessary).

Reducing Complexity

Overbuilding systems is one of the greatest causes of waste in software development. A function that isn't used doesn't just waste the time it took to write it, it makes the system more complex. This makes adding other functionality or fixing existing errors much more time-consuming, not to mention that the system is likely to have more errors in it. By clarifying the scope of work in a clearer way, we can help avoid this.

Other Advantages

If you are building software that must meet government testing specifications (for example, health-care instrumentation), it is easier to prove the software is doing what it needs to if you have a full set of automated acceptance tests. If you just have a set of unit tests (even a complete set), you will still have to demonstrate that your unit tests demonstrate acceptance test criteria. If you are going to have to specify these acceptance tests anyway, you might as well do them first for all the reasons we've been mentioning.

A Comment on Paired Programming
by Alan Shalloway

I have always liked paired programming. I had done things like it but not in a disciplined manner years before I heard of eXtreme Programming. Most people who haven't done it, however, have difficulties seeing why (or how) it would be useful. As an educator (trainer/coach), my work requires not just understanding why something works but knowing how to inform others about why things work. Actually, this is true of all educators but is something we particularly ascribe to at Net Objectives. People readily see the advantage of having several people involved in a conversation about acceptance tests (again, see Chapter 7, Acceptance Test–Driven Development (ATDD)). Paired programming provides somewhat the same advantage at the coding (unit-testing) level.

No Excuses

By the way, there may be certain arguments for not writing and maintaining a set of automated tests. We don't think we would agree with them, or at least, in virtually all cases we are fairly sure we wouldn't. However, there is little argument that can be made for not at least specifying the tests first. This is because you are going to have to specify them at some time. You might as well do it at the time it provides the greatest value.

Summary

There are two kinds of Test-Driven Development: the classic style of writing unit tests first (often called TDD but what we are now calling UTDD) and the more productive method of writing acceptance tests first and then your unit tests (which we are calling ATDD). Both are really about specifying your tests first and then writing the tests, then writing your code, and then running the tests. This creates many advantages. By creating unit tests from the context of your acceptance tests, you will get a better definition of your scope, avoid doing extra work, reduce complexity, and achieve better designs.

CHAPTER 4

Shalloway's Law
and Shalloway's Principle

A few years ago someone in one of my[1] design patterns classes mentioned I should name something after myself since I had written a successful book on design patterns. I, of course, liked this person and his idea immediately. So, I went about thinking about what would be appropriate. The best I could come up with was the following:

> *When N things need to change and N>1, Shalloway will find at most N-1 of these things.*

Although I had hoped to find something complimentary, this was the most appropriate thing I could come up with. I point out that I didn't ask for this when I was born; I was given this "ability." Most people also have this trait. In other words, this isn't choice; it's how we are. This means we had better pay attention to it. Otherwise, we'll find that if we write code that requires finding more than one thing, we won't find them all, but our customers (or if we're lucky, someone else on our team) will.

Although I am not particularly proud of Shalloway's law, I am proud of Shalloway's principle, which I came up with to deal with it. Shalloway's principle states the following:

> *Avoid situations where Shalloway's law applies.*

Kent Beck's famous "once and only once rule" is one approach to this—in other words, keep N at 1—but not the only one. Although avoiding redundancy is perhaps the best way to follow Shalloway's principle, it is not always possible. Let's begin by looking at different types of redundancy and see how we might avoid them, or if not, how we can still follow Shalloway's principle.

---

1. Since this chapter is about Shalloway's law, it is written by Shalloway and therefore is in the first person.

45

Types of Redundancy

If we look at two particular types of redundancy, we can see that although some forms of this pathology are easy to see, others are more subtle. This is important because all forms of redundancy violate Shalloway's principle and create maintenance problems.

Copy and Paste

This is the most obvious type of redundancy and probably the easiest to avoid. Using functions is a common way to avoid this. Rather than copying code from one place to another, we move the code into a function or service class where it can be reused from both places.

Magic Numbers[2]

Using magic numbers as redundancy is not quite as obvious as copy and paste, but it is redundancy. Basically, the redundancy comes from the fact that the meaning of the magic number must be known everywhere the magic number is used. How to avoid magic numbers is well-known—just use #defines or consts or their equivalent, depending upon your language of choice.

Other Types

There are, of course, many other types of redundancy. These include redundant behavior (for example, "save to file" or "save to database"), redundant information, and redundant implementations. We're not going to list them all here. It is important to realize that any time a concept (data, algorithm, code, and so on) appears in more than one place, there is redundancy.

Redefining Redundancy

Redundancy can be much more intricate than what people initially think. The definition of redundancy I am referring to here is "characterized by similarity or repetition."

---

2. Magic numbers are numbers inserted into code that have specific meanings that are not explicitly stated. For example, if the most you can have of something is currently 5 and you have the test refer to "5" explicitly, then 5 is a magic number.

I suggest redundancy can be fairly subtle, and defining it as duplication or repetition is not sufficient. Defining it as similarity, unfortunately, can be a bit vague—so perhaps it isn't that useful either. I propose a definition of redundancy in code that I believe is very useful.

> Redundancy is present if when you make a change in one place in your code, you must make a corresponding change in another place.

A little reflection will tell us that redundancy, at least defined this way, is almost impossible to avoid. For example, a function call has redundancy in it. Both the calling and defined statement must be changed if either change. From this we can also see the relationship between redundancy and coupling. And, as with coupling, not all redundancy is bad or even avoidable. I would say the type of redundancy you must avoid is that redundancy that violates Shalloway's principle.

Redundancy that doesn't violate Shalloway's principle is likely to be a nuisance at most. For example, in the earlier case, I can have a function called from any number of places. Doing so makes my system have a significant amount of redundancy. However, this doesn't violate Shalloway's principle. Why? If I change the defining statement, the compiler will generate a to-do[3] list for me to change my calling statements. I still, of course, have work to make my changes, but that is considerably different from the dangerous situation I would be in if I had to also *find* the changes that were required.

Other Types of Redundancy

Given our new definition of redundancy, what are other common forms of it (and how do we avoid them)? Implementations are often redundant even if the code making them up are not duplicates of each other. For example, if a developer takes a function and copies it (clearly redundant at this point) but then changes all the code (presumably removing the redundancy) because the implementation of the new function is different, do you still have redundancy? I would suggest you do—not of the implementation but most likely the algorithm you are implementing. The second function was copied from the first one presumably because the flow of both algorithms was the same; only their implementations were different.

---

3. The technical term for this to-do list is compilation errors. But I just treat them as a to-do list so I don't have to find them, thereby following Shalloway's principle.

How do you remove this type of redundancy? I'll refer to Chapter 19, The Template Method Pattern, from *Design Patterns Explained: A New Perspective on Object-Oriented Design*. Basically, it involves putting the algorithm in a base (abstract) class and having the implementations of each step be in derived (extended) classes.

The Role of Design Patterns in Reducing Redundancy

We often say that the purpose of design with patterns is to handle variation. Many patterns are readily identified as doing this:

- Strategy handles multiple algorithms.
- Bridge handles multiple implementations.
- Template Method handles multiple implementations of a process.
- Decorator allows for various additional steps in a process.

Most of the design patterns in the seminal work *Design Patterns: Elements of Reusable Object-Oriented Software* (Gamma, Erich, et al. Boston: Addison-Wesley, 1994) are about handling variations directly, or they enable the handling of variations.

Another way to think of design patterns is that they eliminate the redundancy of having to know which implementation is being used.

Because design patterns handle variations in a common manner, they can often be used to eliminate redundant relationships that often exist in a problem domain. For example, a purchasing/selling system will have several types of documents and payment types. Each document type may have a special payment type, but the relationship between them is probably similar to the relationship between any other pair. This sets up redundant relationships. By using abstract classes and interfaces, redundancies can be made explicit and allow the compiler to find things for you. For example, when an interface is used, the compiler will ensure that any new method be defined in all cases—you won't have to go looking for them.

Few Developers Spend a Lot of Time Fixing Bugs

A common misconception among software developers is that they spend a lot of time fixing bugs. But on reflection, most realize that most of their time is spent *finding* the bugs. Actually fixing them takes relatively little time. One of the reasons people spend a lot of time finding bugs is that they have violated Shalloway's principle. If you can't find the cases easily, bugs will result.

A key to avoiding this problem is to be aware of when you are violating Shalloway's principle. Here's an interesting case. Let's say you've been using an Encrypter class in your code. If you've been following our suggestion of separating use from construction, you may have code that looks something like the following:

```
public class BusinessObject {
   public void actionMethod() {
      AnotherObject aAnotherObject= AnotherObject.getInstance()
      String aString;
      String aString2;

      // Other things
      Encrypter myEncrypter= Encrypter.getEncrypter();

      //
      myEncrypter.doYourStuff( aString);

      //
      aAnotherObject( myEncrypter);


      //
      myEncrypter.doYourStuff( aString2);

   }
}

public class AnotherBusinessObject {
   public void actionMethod( Encrypter encrypterToUse) {
      // Other things
      //
      //
      encrypterToUse.doYourStuff( aString);
   }
}
```

Now let's say a case comes up where we don't need to use the Encrypter. We might change the code from

```
// Other things
   Encrypter myEncrypter= Encrypter.getEncrypter();
```

to the following:

```
Encrypter myEncrypter;
If (<<need an encrypter>>)
  myEncrypter= Encrypter.getEncrypter();
```

Then, of course, we have to go through our code and see when we don't have an encrypter.

```
if (myEncrypter != null)
  myEncrypter.doYourStuff( aString);
```

At some point we'll hit the second case of this. This means Shalloway's law is in effect. By the way, a corollary to Shalloway's law is that "If you find two cases, know you won't find all of the cases." At this point, we should figure out a way not to have to test for the null case. An easy way is to put the logic in the getEncrypter method in the first place. In other words, have Encrypter's getEncrypter method consist of the following:

```
// NullEncrypter derives from Encrypter but does no encryption
if (<<don't need an encrypter>>) return new NullEncrypter();
```

This, first of all, keeps all the knowledge about the construction of the encrypter out of the calling class. It also eliminates the need to check for the null condition—both avoiding Shalloway's law and decoupling the client code from the Encrypter object.

This, by the way, is the Null Object Pattern. I suggest that any time you find you are doing a test for null more than once, you should see whether you can use this properly.

I suspect that many readers will think this example is somewhat contrived because with a factory making the Encrypter object, it is pretty clear that the test for a null case should be handled there. But this is also my point—when you separate use from construction, you are more likely to make better decisions later. If getEncrypter wasn't being used and the client code had the rules of construction, setting the myEncrypter reference would likely never occur.

Redundancy and Other Code Qualities

It's useful to note how redundancy is related to other code qualities, in particular, coupling and testability. Any time you have redundancy, it

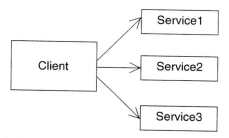

Figure 4.1   Testing in a one-to-many relationship

is likely that if one of the occurrences changes, the other one will need to change. If this is the case, these two cases are coupled. Coupling and redundancy are often different flavors of the same thing.

Note that redundancy also raises the cost of testing. Test cases can often be reduced if redundant relationships are avoided. Let's consider the case shown in Figure 4.1. Note that each of the service objects is doing conceptually the same thing but is doing it in a different way (for example, different kinds of encrypting).

Bain's Corollary and Shalloway's Corollary to Shalloway's Law

When I came up with Shalloway's law, I got some grief from Scott Bain, my friend, compatriot, and critic. I came up with Bain's corollary as an act of vengeance. Bain's corollary says, "When N is large, Bain will find at most N/2!" Unfortunately, I follow Bain's corollary as well. Shalloway's corollary is "When Shalloway is looking for things he has to change and he finds the second case, he knows he won't find them all." (If there are two cases, then N>1.)

Note that we need to have the following for a full set of tests:

- Test of `Service1`
- Test of `Service2`
- Test of `Service3`
- `Client` using `Service1`

- Client using `Service2`

- Client using `Service3`

The need for testing `Client` using the services is because we have no assurance that we've abstracted out the service code. There may be coupling taking place, especially since each service interface may be different. Notice what happens when more clients become involved—this gets worse and worse.

Now, consider what happens if we make sure that all the service objects work in the same way. In this case, we basically abstract out the service objects. If we put in an abstraction layer (either an abstract class or an interface that the services implement), we get what is shown in Figure 4.2.

Although we still need to test each `Service`, we now need to test only the `Client` to `Service` relationship. Note that as we get more client objects the savings are even greater.

Summary

Shalloway's law is both a humorous attempt at saying avoid redundancy and some guidance for developers in how to do so—or at least to make it less costly not to do so. Understanding redundancy is key to Shalloway's law, and avoiding the cost of it is the essence of Shalloway's principle.

A powerful question when programming that can be deduced from all of this is "If this changes, how many places will I have to change things, and can the compiler find those for me?" If you can't see a way to make it so the answer is either "1" or "yes," then you have to acknowledge that you have a less than ideal design. At this point, you should consider an alternative—or, heaven help you—ask someone else to suggest an alternative.

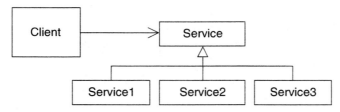

Figure 4.2   Creating a one-to-one relationship

CHAPTER 5

Encapsulate That!

"Encapsulation" is a word that's been with us in software development for a long time, but if you asked people what it means, many would say something like "hiding data." In fact, there are quite a few books and websites that would use that as the definition of the word. However, we have found that an examination of the true meaning of encapsulation can be enormously beneficial and can make many other aspects of object-oriented (OO) design (design patterns, for instance) easier to understand and to use.

We begin simply, by showing encapsulation in its most obvious and straightforward forms, and then expand these concepts into the patterns and all the qualities of code that make it fundamentally easier to maintain, debug, enhance, and scale. What you will see is that encapsulation, given its more useful definition, is a fundamental, first principle of OO.

Unencapsulated Code: The Sabotage of the Global Variable

The following is the lowest degree of encapsulation possible in a pure-OO language like Java or C#.

```
public class Foo {
  public static int x;
}
```

Any class in the system can access x, either to use its value in a calculation or other process (and thus become dependent upon it) or to alter its value (and thus cause a side effect in those classes that depend on it). Foo.x might as well be thought of as Global.x (and in fact there are many developers who have done just this), and in one fell swoop the efforts of the Java and C# creators to prevent global variables are thwarted.

Global variables are ineffective because they create tight coupling. They are rather like a doorknob that everyone in the household touches and, thus, during the cold and flu season becomes the vector for sharing germs. If any class in the system can depend on Foo.x and if any other class can change it, then in theory every class is potentially coupled to every other class, and unless your memory is perfect, you're likely to forget some of these links when maintaining the code. The errors that creep in over time will often be devilishly difficult to find. We'd like to prevent things that carry such obvious potential for pain.

What most OO developers would naturally think of as the lowest degree of encapsulation is the following:

```
public class Foo{
   public int x;
}
```

That x in this case is an instance variable is, in fact, a kind of encapsulation. Now, for any class in the system to depend on x, it must have a reference to an instance of Foo, and for two classes to be coupled to each other through x, they must both have a reference to the *same* instance of Foo.

A number of techniques can prevent this from happening, so whereas a public static variable cannot be encapsulated, here we have at least a chance of preventing unintended side effects. There are weakly typed languages that posit this level of encapsulation to be enough in and of itself.

Also note that Foo is a public class. Another encapsulating action would be to remove the `public` keyword, which would mean that only classes in the same package (Java) or assembly (C#) would be able to access Foo in any way at all.

Encapsulation of Member Identity

Although putting x into an instance does create some degree of encapsulation, it fails to create an encapsulation of identity.

Identity is the principle of existence. Identity coupling is usually thought of in terms of class A "knowing" that class B exists (usually by having a member of its type, taking a parameter of its type, or returning its type from a method), but instance variables have identity, too.

The following puts it another way:

```
public class Foo {
   public int x;
}

public class Bar {
   private Foo myFoo = new Foo();
   public int process(){
     int intialValue = myFoo.x;
     return initialValue * 4;
   }
}
```

Ignoring that this particular implementation of `Bar`'s `process()` method would consistently produce a zero, note that not only is `Bar` coupled to the value of `x` in the instance pointed to by `myFoo`, but it is also coupled to the fact that `x` is an integer (or, at minimum, a type that can be implicitly cast to one) and that it is an instance member of the `Foo` class. It is coupled to `x`'s nature.

If a future revision of `Foo` requires that `x` be stored as, for instance, a String, that it be obtained from a database or remote connection dynamically at runtime, or that it be calculated from other values whenever it is asked for, then `Bar`'s method of accessing it will have to change. `Bar` will have to change because `Foo` changed (and so will every other class that accesses `x` in a `Foo` instance). This is unnecessary coupling.

Encapsulating the identity of `x` requires that we create a method or methods that encapsulate `x`'s nature.

```
public class Foo {
   private int x;
   public int getX() {
     return x;
   }
   public void setX(int anInt){
     x = anInt;
   }
}

public class Bar {
   private Foo mFoo = new Foo();
   public int process(){
     int intialValue = myFoo.getX();
     return initialValue * 4;
   }
}
```

The new way of accessing Foo's x in Bar (highlighted in bold) now creates an encapsulation of x's identity, or nature. Bar is coupled only to the fact that getX() in Foo takes no parameters and returns an integer, not that x is actually stored as a integer, or that it's actually stored in Foo, or that it's stored anywhere at all (it could be a random number).

Now the developers are free to change Foo without affecting Bar, or any other class that calls getX(), so long as they don't change the method signature.

```
public class Foo {
   public String x = "0"; // x no longer an int
   public int getX() {
     // convert when needed
     return Integer.parseInt(x);
   }
   public void setX(int anInt){
     // convert back
     x = new Integer(anInt).toString();
   }
}

public class Bar {
   private Foo mFoo = new Foo();
   public int process(){
     // none the wiser
     int intialValue = myFoo.getX();
     return initialValue * 4;
   }
}
```

Here x is now stored as a String (though this is just one of any number of changes that could be made to the way x is maintained in Foo), but Bar need not be touched at all.

Why?

What you hide, you can change. The fact that x was an integer in Foo was hidden, so it could be changed. Envisioning this over and over again throughout a system leads to the conclusion that the power to make changes, to make extensions, and to fix bugs is made much easier when you encapsulate as much and as often as possible.

Self-Encapsulating Members

Although many developers might find it quite natural to encapsulate a data member behind a set of accessor methods (another word for get()

and set() methods), the standard practice for accessing a data member from within the class itself is generally to refer to it directly.

```
public class Foo{
  private int x;
  public int getX(){
    return x;
  }
  public void setX(int anInt){
    x = anInt;
  }
  public boolean isPrime(){
    boolean rval = true;
    for(int i=2; i<(x/2); i++){
      if(Math.mod(i, x) == 0)
        rval = false;
    }
      return rval;
    }
}
```

Here, isPrime() calculates a true/false condition on x, which is local to Foo(), so even though x is private, it can be accessed directly in the method.

For the most part it's a matter of convenience, but consider the earlier scenario where Foo was changed to the effect that x is no longer stored as an int or is no longer stored as a local data member at all (perhaps it's stored in a database, serialized to the disk, obtained from some other class, or calculated from other values). Now isPrime(), and any other local method that directly refers to x, will have to be rewritten to account for the new situation. In fact, the new code in local methods that converts whatever x has become into the integer it used to be will likely be highly redundant. And we know we don't want redundancy.

However, for the most part it's a matter of convenience, but if the possibility of x changing in this way seems likely (what Bruce Eckel calls "the anticipated vector of change"), then using getX() even within Foo's own methods would reduce the maintenance headaches considerably when the change is made.

You have to weigh the syntactic inconvenience of writing getX() instead of x in these algorithms against the need to make extensive changes when and if the nature of x needs to change. Generally, it's found to be worth the extra typing.

Preventing Changes

Another advantage of the accessor methods shown earlier is the capability to make a member of a class "read-only." If we simply remove the setX() method in Foo earlier, then the value is readable but not changeable. This eliminates the potential that Foo may serve to couple two other classes, since although one class may depend on the return value of getX(), no other class may change this value.

Alternately, we could eliminate the getX() method but leave setX(), meaning that another class could change the state of a Foo instance, but none could depend on it.

.NET has instituted an alternative way of accomplishing this, called a property:

```
// C#
public class Foo {
  private int myX;
  public int x {
    get { return myX; }
    // 'value' is an implicit variable
    set { myX = value; }
  }
}
```

This is a bit of syntactic sugar that allows the programmer to embed the gets and sets as part of the data-member definition. Bar, however, would still access it like it would any public variable.

```
// C#
public class Bar {
  private Foo mFoo = new Foo();
  public int process(){
    // actually calls the get
    int intialValue = myFoo.x;
    return initialValue * 4;
  }
}
```

The theory here is that x could have begun its life as a public member and then later could be changed to a property without changing Bar. In Foo, you could eliminate the set{} code like before to make the property read-only (or the get{} to make it write-only) or could write them to fetch/send/calculate x and thus gain similar beneficial encapsulation as was possible with the getX() and setX() methods.

There are arguments to be made for and against this. We won't engage in them here, but the good news is that, in C#, you can use either technique easily. Note that self-encapsulating a data member is a simpler issue in C#, because the syntax for referencing the member locally would not have to be changed when the member became a property.

The Difficulty of Encapsulating Reference Objects

One common practice in OO is the use of constructors to guarantee the proper creation of contained objects. Consider the following code.

```
public Foo{
  private int x;
  // Constructor requires an int be passed in
  Foo (int anInt){
    x = anInt;
  }
  public int getX() {
    return x;
  }
  public void setX(int newInt) {
    x = newInt;
  }
}

public Bar{
  private Foo myFoo;
  // Constructor requires an instance of Foo
  public Bar(Foo aFoo){
    myFoo = aFoo;
  }
  public int process(){
    int intialValue = myFoo.getX();
    return initialValue * 4;
  }
}
public class Client{
  public static void main(String[] args){
    int x = 5; // Make needed int for Foo instance
    Foo f = new Foo(x); // Made Foo instance using x
    Bar b = new Bar(f); // Make Bar instance using f
    int i = b.process();// Use Bar instance
  }
}
```

Here Client creates an instance of Foo (initializing the value of x by passing an int into the constructor) and then hands this instance to the Bar constructor, which the instance of Bar will now hold as a private member.

Is myFoo in Bar encapsulated? It's private. It has no set() method to allow changes to it (it does not even have a get() method). Isn't the concept of a private member with no accessors the very definition of member encapsulation? The assumption most developers would make is that myFoo is fully encapsulated, and this could be a disastrous assumption.

Consider the following version of the Client class.

```
public class Client{
  public static void main(String[] args){
    int x = 5;
    Foo f = new Foo(x);
    Bar b = new Bar(f);
    int i = b.process();
    f.setX(10); // Still holding the Foo reference!
    i = b.process();
  }
}
```

b.process() will produce an entirely different value in the second call, because Client still holds a reference to f (the instance of Foo it created to hand over to Bar's constructor) and thus can still change its state. We call this effect "aliasing." Since Bar's behavior depends upon the state of this Foo reference, Client can break the encapsulation if it retains this Foo reference for its own purposes, and Bar cannot prevent it from doing so. If Client passes this Foo reference to another class, then it, too, will be able to break the encapsulation of myFoo in Bar.

This is because myFoo is a reference to an object on the heap. When Client calls new Bar(f), f is indeed passed by copy, but it's a copy of a reference, and it therefore points to the same instance that the original did, so the copying neither hides nor protects it from future manipulation. Contrast this with the call to new Foo(x). Since x is a value, not a reference, the copying of x completely removes any possibility that Client can change it by changing the original. In the following code fragment

```
int x = 5;
Foo f = new Foo(x);
x = 10;
```

the code x = 10 will have no effect on the state of f, because the integer it holds is a different integer than the one Client has. It's a copy.

So, this problem of altering-after-the-fact is unique to references (at least in Java) and can be tricky to deal with. One way of solving the problem is by having Bar make a defensive copy of the Foo reference it takes in its constructor, assuring that it holds a different reference of Foo (with the same state) than any other object holds. This requires that Foo be cloneable or that it exposes its state so that Bar can make another Foo with the same state. Let's examine two versions of Bar's constructor that could ensure good encapsulation of its myFoo member.

```
public Bar(Foo aFoo){
  myFoo = new Foo(aFoo.getX());
}
```

This will work as the code is written because aFoo allows Bar, an outside class, to access its x member, and so Bar can make a new, private, separate Foo for its own use. Now Client can manipulate the original Foo all it wants and will not affect Bar.

If Foo did not allow this access (if it had no getX() method), then Foo could be made cloneable:

```
public class Foo{
  private int x;
  public Foo(int anInt){
    x = anInt;
  }
  public Foo clone(){
    return new Foo(x);
  }
}
```

and so Bar's constructor could make its defensive copy in the following way:

```
public Bar(Foo aFoo){
  myFoo = aFoo.clone();
}
```

Either way, Bar's myFoo reference will point to a different object on the heap than any other class in the system, and thus myFoo is once again completely encapsulated.

Breaking Encapsulation with Get()

Making members private and then providing get() methods but no set() methods is often thought to be strong encapsulation.

We saw earlier how this is not the case with reference objects. However, if we take the step of making a defensive copy of any reference held by a particular class, then can we still say that set() methods break encapsulation but get() methods do not? A set() allows an outside class to make a change, but a get() does not, right?

Not with references. Consider the following:

```
public Bar{
  private Foo myFoo;
  public Bar(Foo aFoo){
    myFoo = aFoo.clone(); // Make a private instance
  }
  public Foo getFoo(){
    return myFoo;
  }
  public int process(){
    int intialValue = myFoo.getX();
    return initialValue * 4;
  }
}

public class Client{
  public static void main(String[] args){
    int x = 5;
    Foo f = new Foo(x);
    // Bar will make a defensive copy
    Bar b = new Bar(f);
    int i = b.process();
    // Client gets Bar's new Foo.
    Foo fFromBar = b.getFoo();
    fFromBar.setX(10); // ...and changes it
    i = b.process(); // effecting Bar again.
  }
}
```

Here Client makes a Foo, and Bar clones it to defend against subsequent manipulation by Client. However, Client is able to get Bar's newly made, private Foo reference by calling the getFoo() method provided, so encapsulation is broken again. The only way around this is to have Bar clone myFoo again and then return this object from its getFoo() method.

```
public Bar{
  private Foo myFoo;
  public Bar(Foo aFoo){
    myFoo = aFoo.clone();
  }
  public Foo getFoo(){
    // Return a clone, not the member
    return myFoo.clone();
  }
  public int process(){
    int intialValue = myFoo.getX();
    return initialValue * 4;
  }
}
```

If a setFoo() method is provided, it would have to work like the constructor does to ensure the encapsulation is maintained. So, the game is completely different when dealing with value objects (which are themselves passed by copy) and reference objects (which are references passed by copy).

Put another way, an entity that appears to be strongly encapsulated but that contains references that are not encapsulated really isn't as encapsulated as it appears. We always need to ask ourselves how changes from the outside can affect a given class and see encapsulation as a protection against those changes. Table 5.1 shows the different degrees of encapsulation achieved with value and reference types.

C# makes this issue both simpler and more complex.

For instance, although the only value objects in Java are the primitives (int, float, boolean, and the like), in C# it is possible to create value objects with both complex state and functional members (methods),

Table 5.1   Encapsulation of Value and Reference Types

Activity	Value Object Encapsulation?	Reference Object Encapsulation?
State passed into constructor	Yes	No, unless a defensive copy is made
Get() method provided	Yes	No, unless a defensive copy is returned
Set() method provided	No	No, unless a defensive copy is made

called "structs." Structs work very much like classes do (you can instantiate them, and they can implement interfaces), but they are passed by making complete copies of the object, not by copying a reference to an instance, so these particular encapsulation issues can be largely alleviated.

However, C# also makes value objects passable by reference, using `ref` and `out` keywords in method signatures, so it's possible to break encapsulation on any member, value, or reference, if they are used. Therefore, `ref` and `out` should be used very carefully.

A pragmatic point is that with all these issues, the main danger comes when you break encapsulation unknowingly. Many approaches to design might take advantage of the fact that a reference passed into a constructor could subsequently be used to change state on a contained object or that a value object in C# could be externalized through a `ref` or an `out` parameter. If this is intentional and well-documented, then the danger is minimal.

However, these subtle issues can easily escape notice and create situations where members seem to be well-encapsulated and yet are not. Understanding how and why this happens is the best defense.

Even When Done Correctly, Getters and Setters Break Encapsulation

So far we've talked about how getters and setters can inadvertently break encapsulation. But there is a subtle way they violate encapsulation even when used properly. This is that they expose that the concept is part of the containing class. In other words, if there is a `getX` in `Foo`, even if it does not expose how `x` is implemented in `Foo`, entities will become coupled to the fact that `Foo` has a concept called `x` (and how to use it). It's better to hide the concept entirely if possible.

Encapsulation of Object Type

Encapsulation is often thought of as data hiding. There are even references that define it as precisely that. However, encapsulation is a broader notion; as we've already seen, it's meaningful to think of encapsulating the identity of a data member, not just the value that it holds.

Taken further, it's possible to think of the hiding of entire object types as encapsulation as well. The following is an example.

```
public abstract class Calculator{
  public abstract int calc(int x, int y);
}

public class Adder extends Calculator{
  public int calc(int x, int y) {
    return x + y;
  }
}

public class Multiplier extends Calculator{
  public int calc(int x, int y){
    return x * y;
  }
}
```

Here, `Adder` and `Multiplier` extend the abstract base class `Calculator`. Because of this, any instance of `Adder` or `Multiplier` can be held by a reference of `Calculator` type (this is called an "implicit cast"), and the class that holds the reference need not "know" what is "really" being held. The following is an example.

```
public class CalcUser{
  private Calculator myCalculator;
  public CalcUser(Calculator aCalculator){
    myCalculator = aCalculator;
  }
  public void process(){
    int i1 = 4;
    int i2 = 5;
    int r = myCalculator.calc(i1, i2);
  }
}
```

Note that `CalcUser` contains no mention whatsoever of `Adder` or `Multiplier`, yet `Calculator` itself is abstract (cannot be instantiated), so whatever instance is passed into the constructor will have to be either an instance of `Adder` or an instance of `Multiplier` (these are the only classes that can be cast to `Calculator`, so the type checking in the compiler will allow only these instances to be passed in).

Since they share a common interface, `CalcUser` can use either `Adder` or `Multiplier` instances in exactly the same way (this is an example of polymorphism) without any knowledge of which subclass it has, even what subclasses are possible, or even that `Calculator` is abstract in the first place.

This is the encapsulation of object type. `Calculator`, an abstract base class (although this is equally true if an interface is used), encapsulates its subclasses if other classes hold their references to them as an upcast to the base type. Most of the popular design patterns make use of this, and it is just what the "Gang of Four" had in mind when they made the recommendation[1] that good designers should "design to interfaces."

It's a tad more complicated in C# because, unlike Java, methods in C# are not automatically virtual (late-bound). This means a method called on a subclass reference that was cast back to the superclass type may revert to the superclass method unless the `override` keyword is used in the subclass method.

```
public abstract class Calculator{
  // abstract methods are inherently virtual
  public abstract int calc(int x, int y);
}

public class Adder : Calculator{
  public override int calc(int x, int y) {
    return x + y;
  }
}
public class Multiplier : Calculator{
  public override int calc(int x, int y){
    return x * y;
  }
}
```

Note that `calc()` is abstract in `Calculator`, and so it is inherently/automatically virtual. Sometimes base classes provide default implementations of methods, and if these are present, they must be declared virtual, or they may not be overridden like the following:

```
public abstract class Calculator{
  // default implementation must be 'virtual'
  public virtual int calc(int x, int y){
    return System.Math.Max(x, y);
  }
}
```

1. Gamma, Erich, Richard Helm, Robert Johnson, and John M. Vlissides. *Design Patterns: Elements of Reusable Object-Oriented Software.* Reading, MA: Addison-Wesley, 1994.

Encapsulation of Design

In the previous example, the `Calculator` abstraction made it possible to hide the specific kinds of calculator subclasses that exist from other parts of the application.

The virtue of this is maintainability and flexibility; we can add new types of calculators to the system without changing the client objects that use them.

However, whereas we can hide the specific classes `Adder` and `Multiplier` from most of the rest of the system, certainly we cannot hide them entirely. Something, somewhere, will have to contain the code new `Adder()` and new `Multiplier()` in order for these classes to be instantiated. And, something will have to make the decision as to which one to build in a given circumstance. If the client objects that use these classes are given this responsibility, then we must break the encapsulation of type, and we lose the modularity that seemed so attractive.

The obvious answer is to use another object to build the `Calculator` subclasses.

Such an object is usually called an "object factory."

```
public class CalculatorFactory {
  public Calculator getCalculator() {
    if(someDecision()) {
      return new Adder();
    } else {
      return new Multiplier();
    }
  }
}
```

If all other objects that require a `Calculator` implementation use this factory to get it, then we have one single place to maintain when a new class, say, `Subtractor`, comes into being.

In *Design Patterns: Elements of Reusable Object-Oriented Software*, the authors[2] illustrate the encapsulation of type in many of their patterns, such as the Strategy Pattern.

```
public class Client {
  public static void main(String[] args) {
    Context c = new context();
    Strategy s = StrategyFactory.getStrategy();
```

---

2. Gamma, Erich, Richard Helm, Robert Johnson, and John M. Vlissides. *Design Patterns: Elements of Reusable Object-Oriented Software*. Reading, MA: Addison-Wesley, 1994

```
      c.takeAction(s);
  }
}
public class Context {
  public void takeAction(Strategy myStrategy) {
    // Whatever else
    myStrategy.varyingAction();
    // Whatever else
  }
}
pubic abstract class Strategy {
  public abstract void varyingAction;
}
```

StrategyFactory (not shown) clearly makes an implementing subclass (also not shown) of Strategy and provides this to Client. Then Client hands this to the Context object to use. Context is "unaware" of which actual Strategy implementation it has, and so is Client, since it obtained it from the StrategyFactory blindly.

But there is still an opportunity for encapsulation here that we're not taking advantage of. The Strategy implementations are hidden from everything except StrategyFactory, but Client does have "awareness" of the fact that the Context object requires a Strategy implementation to be "handed in" in order to function properly. What is not encapsulated, therefore, is the Strategy Pattern itself, the design we're using to handle the variation. If at some point in the future we decide to change this design to one where no such delegation takes place or where the delegation is accomplished in some other way, then we'll have to change the way Client interacts with Context. The design is not encapsulated.

Sometimes this is necessary. If, for instance, we need a high degree of dynamism in the way Context operates (perhaps every time it is used we need to be able to give it a different Strategy implementation), then this implementation of the pattern would be appropriate. Where it is not necessary, however, it's better to hide the design.

How? The most common techniques to either

- Have the Context object request the Strategy implementation from StrategyFactory, instead of having Client do so. Thereby, Client can simply call the method on Context without handing anything in.

- Have a factory build the Context object in the first place and while doing so hand in the proper Strategy object via its constructor.

Or we can do both. Let a factory establish the initial `Strategy` to use but let the `Context` object (or the `Client`) change this when/as needed. Either way, the `Client` object would now have no coupling to the fact that the Strategy Pattern was in use, which would make it much easier to change this design when/if the issues involved became more complex and this design was no longer adequate.

Encapsulation on All Levels

We should strive to encapsulate everything that can be encapsulated, because it simplifies maintenance every time we do so. Also, it is always easy to break encapsulation after the fact than to encapsulate something later. When something is encapsulated and a need arises that requires the hidden thing to be revealed, we simply provide access. When something was not encapsulated and now needs to be hidden, then every part of the application that has become coupled to it must be reworked.

To achieve maximum encapsulation, you must do the following:

- Encapsulate by policy, reveal by need. When in doubt, hide it, and then reveal it when this becomes necessary.

- Broaden your view of what can be hidden. Using an object factory, for instance, encapsulates the construction issue and can even encapsulate an entire design, if all the players in the solution are built by the factory. We don't normally think of this as "encapsulation," but it is, and it brings the same value that other types of encapsulation bring: ease of change later.

Practical Advice: Encapsulate Your Impediments

We are, among other things, consultants and coaches at Net Objectives. Very often, our role is to help people find a good solution to a problem they are having, and often that solution will be one of the many well-known design patterns that have been documented in our industry.

In other words, sometimes it is a matter of *selecting* a good pattern to use, at least as a starting point, to reveal a natural and powerful solution to the problem before us.

What we noticed, over time, was that the interaction between the coach and the customer had a certain repetition to it. It would often go something like the following:

Customer: I have problem so and so, and I'm not sure what to do.

Coach: Describe the problem, and I'll see whether I can help.

Customer: (long description)

Coach: Can you boil that down a bit? What's the aspect of this that really is causing you the problem?

Customer: (shorter description, still hard to see)

Coach: Focus your description a little more. Try to get to the one big thing that you're concerned about.

Customer: (one or two sentences that describe the major impediment)

Coach: Encapsulate that!

Of course, the conversation never literally goes this way, but in one form or another, as a coach, we always seem to be suggesting that something be encapsulated.

How does this help?

Many, many things can be encapsulated, and in each case, the technique used to encapsulate a given thing is almost always a design pattern. In our simple example earlier about the various calculators, the "thing being encapsulated" is the calculation algorithm. The Strategy Pattern does that; it encapsulates a single varying algorithm.

The other patterns encapsulate things like the following:

- Sequences

- Relationships

- Multiple varying algorithms

- Dependent varying algorithms

- Creation of complex objects

- Structures of objects

So, if you can figure out what your problem is and where your biggest risks and concerns are, you might not be able to solve them, but you may be able to limit their impact by encapsulating them.

See www.netobjectivesrepository.com/PatternsByEncapsulation for a cross-index at our Design Patterns Repository, listing patterns by what they encapsulate.

Encapsulate That! in Practice

Seeking to encapsulate is something that many developers have learned from their experiences, in different ways and under different circumstances. Here is one such experience, as related by Al Shalloway.

I have learned that asking good questions is often a very good design technique. One of my favorite questions when I am designing code is the following: "If I knew that however I was going to figure this out now was going to need to change in an unexpected way in the future, how would I design it?"

This is a subtle question. I am somewhat acting as if no matter what I do will be wrong. This is not pessimistic as much as it is realistic. I am what I call "precognitive impaired." I don't do precognition. However, I can take advantage of experience. Although I don't know how my requirements are going to change (this would require precognition), I do know that they will change (this is experience). I also know, from experience, that if I design for something to occur, it may not. If I added things to my design that are now not needed, I have added complexity to my code for likely no gain.

I am asking the question, how do we design when we know that we don't yet know all we need to make a good design? My answer is to encapsulate the concept that we have uncertainty about. This follows our general mantra of encapsulating by policy, reveal by need. Let's see an example of how this works.

I was talking to a client once who was working on a system that had several processors in it. Each of these processors often had events that other processors needed to know about. The question was, how should they communicate with each other? The need for a `Messaging` class was clear, but how should it be implemented? First in line for consideration was a `Messenger` class that used TCP/IP. There were other candidates as well. The concern was that performance was going to be critical, but at the start of the project, without complete software to measure, it was difficult to tell what the performance problem really was going to be.

continues

I was being asked to solve a problem that required knowledge that wasn't available now. I, of course, could guess or use my experience, but in fact, my experience told me that this was an approach that hadn't led to a lot of success for me. Stated another way, my experience was that whatever I decided upon now was going to be discovered to be wrong in the future.

The approach to take, of course, is to encapsulate the Messenger class. That is, build a class to do messaging knowing we are going to have to rewrite it after we discover how we should have built it. Now this may seem like a lot of waste, but it actually isn't. If we take the attitude that we are going to rewrite this messaging object, it's probable that we can find a really simple one to write at first. It's also possible we can mock the object. If our messaging is merely used to tell other objects on different processors things and we are not getting messages back, then a write-only mock works quite well and is trivial to write.

In any event, I suggest that a real message object would not be that difficult to write. Bear in mind that while we are working on our code and haven't delivered it yet, we can take several short-cuts as long as we have prepared for them. For example, we might write a TCP/IP message handler without full error handling. We can throw exceptions when an error occurs, intending to write the error handling later (if we, indeed, keep TCP/IP at all).

Summary

In writing their groundbreaking book on patterns, the "Gang of Four" had several pieces of general design advice for us. Among these was a phrase that is sometimes dismissed as "old thinking" because of the way it is worded.

> *Consider what should be variable in your design and encapsulate the concept that varies.*

Perhaps because of the word "should," this can be interpreted as a "big design up-front" point of view; indeed, it likely was written to mean that, given that the book was written in 1994 at a time when this was the predominant way of thinking about software design.

However, we have learned to see design as a constant process, and we do not expect to be able to anticipate every design element we will need before we begin to create a product. In other words, we don't trust our ability to know, consistently and reliably, what "should" be variable. So, the advice we would give is very similar, with just a small change of focus.

> Consider what is now, or about to become, varying, and encapsulate it conceptually.

In the past it was seen as dangerous to wait on such decisions, but if we follow good practices such as "Programming by Intention" and encapsulating construction and if we define our tests early, we find that the risks of waiting are largely removed, and we can work in a more responsive, reality-based way.

That said, it is good to discover what you can, especially mission-critical issues, as early as you can. This also can help us avoid/remove the risk of deferring commitment to a specific design. One practice that can help you here is "Commonality-Variability Analysis," which is the subject of Chapter 10.

CHAPTER 6

Interface-Oriented Design

Interface-oriented design (IOD) concentrates on the services and responsibilities of objects or modules, rather than their implementation. It cleanly separates the specification perspective from the implementation perspective. IOD is applicable to both object-oriented systems and non-object-oriented systems.[1]

Design to Interfaces

The Gang of Four[2] recommends that you should "design to interfaces, not implementations." Many patterns, such as the Adapter, Façade, Strategy, and Proxy deal with interfaces. Martin Fowler[3] repeats this in his recommondation of separating the specification perspective (the interface) from the implementation perspective. Interfaces are the key to making decoupled designs that simplify testing and promote maintainability.

Definition of Interface

What is an interface? In common terms, it is the way to interact with another entity—a method, a class, a module, or a program. Common forms of interfaces are the following:

- An object's set of accessible methods

- A protocol, such as File Transfer Protocol (FTP) or Simple Mail Transfer Protocol (SMTP)

- A programmatic interface, such as a web service

---

1. Pugh, Ken. *Interface-Oriented Design*. Raleigh, NC: Pragmatic Bookshelf, 2006.
2. Gamma, Erich, Richard Helm, Ralph Johnson, and John M. Vlissides. *Design Patterns: Elements of Reusable Object-Oriented Software*. Reading, MA: Addison-Wesley, 1994.
3. See http://martinfowler.com.

The public methods of an object are deemed its interface. An interface can also be specifically defined in language-specific terms. For example, in Java and C#, you can declare an interface construct using the keyword `interface`. The interface consists of a set of method signatures (name, parameters, return type, and exceptions that may be thrown). Interfaces do not have data members (attributes), because that would imply an implementation.[4]

An interface can be a set of textual commands, rather than method calls. For example, with FTP, you ask for a listing of a directory by using the `LIST` command. You get a particular file with the `RETR` (retrieve) command.[5] You can write an adapter that converts this textual interface to the method calls in a particular language.

A web service has an interface defined in Web Services Description Language (WSDL). It describes the operations performed by a web service, the type (for example, one-way or request-response), and the data types involved.

Interface Contracts

Every interface should have an explicit contract such as Bertrand Meyer's "Design by Contract."[6] The contract includes the preconditions and postconditions. Preconditions are things that must be true when an operation is invoked, such as a file being open. Postconditions are that which will be true after the operation is finished, such as data being written to a file. The contract also encompasses the protocol—the sequence in which various operations in an interface are called to perform a particular behavior.

The tests for an interface clarify its contract. The tests may be sequentially developed in conjunction with developing an implementation (as in Test-Driven Development) or created prior to any implementation (as in Acceptance Test–Driven Development). If you are requesting another group to develop an implementation for an interface, it is your responsibility to provide the acceptance tests for that interface.

---

4. C# allows interfaces to have properties. In C++, a class with all pure virtual methods and no data members is equivalent to an interface. The template method construct in C++ can also be considered equivalent to an interface.
5. User-level FTP programs let you type `ls` to get the list or `get` followed by the name of the file to retrieve the file. These user commands are translated into these FTP commands.
6. Meyer, Bertrand. *Object-Oriented Software Construction*. Upper Saddle River, NJ: Prentice Hall, 1997.

Passing the tests indicates that an implementation fulfills its contracts. Functional contract tests are usually automated to ensure that implementation changes (for example, refactoring) do not affect its contract. Other contract tests may be manual or automated. For example, an implementation may need to pass the "ility" tests, such as reliability, scalability, or performance tests as well.

Ken Pugh's book *Interface-Oriented Design* describes three laws of interfaces (adapted from Asimov's *I Robot*). The first is that an interface's implementation shall do what its methods say it does. This law is related to Programming by Intention as well as having intention-revealing names (see Chapter 1, Programming by Intention). The law is enforced by the functional tests for an implementation. The second law is that an interface implementation must do no harm. This corresponds to the "ility" tests. For example, it should not consume large amounts of resources unless absolutely essential to its operation. The third is that if an implementation is unable to perform its responsibilities, it must notify its caller. This relates to negative functional testing in that you set up conditions for failure and check that the operation actually reports failure. It doesn't matter the form of the failure report—an error code or a thrown exception.

Separating Perspectives

Martin Fowler suggests that you separate the specification (interface) perspective from the implementation perspective. Using interfaces in your design forces that separation. For example, suppose you need to look up a customer. You could put some SQL code into a module and execute that code on the server. Or you could create an interface, such as the following:[7]

```
interface CustomerLookup {
  Customer getCustomerByID(ID anID);
}
```

Following the third law, you need to specify (preferably with tests) what should occur if a customer is not found with anID. Is the return value going to be NULL, or is some type of exception (say Customer-NotFound) going to be thrown?

---

7. C# uses the convention of having an I before the name of an interface. So, this would be called ICustomerLookup. If that is prevalent in your development environment, then be consistent with that convention.

The interface can be fulfilled by going to a server-provided database and getting the information. Alternatively, it could be an in-memory database. It also could be implemented by reading an XML file whose name indicated that it contained information on the customer with anID. You might even have an implementation send a request to a human clerk to look up the information in a paper file, type it in, and transmit it back.[8]

```
class DataBaseCustomerLookup implements CustomerLookup {
  Customer getCustomerByID(ID anID){
    // create SQL for lookup
  }
}
class XMLCustomerLookup implements CustomerLookup {
  Customer getCustomerByID(ID anID){
    // open and read file with name <anID>.data
  }
}
```

Separating perspectives allows easy substitutions of implementations during testing. For interfaces whose production implementation may take a relatively long time to execute (for example, databases), create a mock implementation for testing. Based on the testing needs, the mock could act as a simple returner of fixed values or an in-memory replica that can insert and delete records.

Another separation of perspective is decoupling the external representation from the internal implementation. Internal logic should not be dependent upon external format. For data interfaces, create a class that represents the data.[9] Then provide methods to export and import externally formatted data to and from that class. For interfaces that are textual, create an adapter that allows programmatic control. For example, the FTP protocol could have an adapter such as the following:

```
class FTP {
  Boolean connect(String host, String username,
    String password) {
    // Connects to host with username and password
  }
  String [] list() {
    // issues the LIST command and returns list of files
  }
```

---

8. This might have an impact on the application's performance.
9. This is sometimes termed a data transfer object (DTO).

```
Boolean get(String filename) {
  // issues RETR <filename> command
  // creates file
  // returns false if file not found
}
}
```

Along the same lines, you can separate your programmatic internal interface from an API that is supplied by an external vendor or development group. Create the interface you want and then adapt it (through the Adapter or Façade Pattern) to the actual interface.

Mock Implementations of Interfaces

Interfaces provide a distinct point where a mock or test double can be inserted for unit testing.[10] The mock can be controlled by the test to provide appropriate responses, to check that the unit under test makes the appropriate calls, or to do both.

If an implementation of an API is not available or is relatively slow, then you can develop a mock implementation of the interface you created for it, as in the previous section. This will probably be easier than mocking out the entire API. You often use only a small portion of an API, and the contract tests will be much smaller in number.[11]

Keep Interfaces Simple

Keep interfaces simple. They should have the minimum number of methods needed to get the job done. If you need more complex operations, implement them by delegating to simple interfaces. This cuts down on testing for each interface. The FTP interface described previously handles getting files one at a time. If you need to get multiple files that match a wildcard pattern, do not add that as a method in the FTP interface. Instead, create a class, such as the one shown here, that uses the FTP interface. This is a practical variation of the Open-Closed principle (see Chapter 11). The original interface is closed for modification but open for extension by delegating to it.

---

10. See Mackinnon, Tim, Steve Freeman, and Philip Craig. "EndoTesting: Unit Testing with Mock Objects." www.mockobjects.com/files/endotesting.pdf, as well as Meszaros, Gerard. *xUnit Test Patterns: Refactoring Test Code*. Boston, MA: Addison-Wesley, 2007.

11. See Chapter 12, Needs versus Capabilities Interfaces.

```
class ExtendedFTP {
  void multiple_get(String wildcard_pattern ) {
    // calls FTP.list() to obtain list of files
    // calls FTP.get() for each file in list
    //    that matches the pattern
  }
}
```

Avoids Premature Hierarchies

Polymorphism is a key principle in object-oriented design. You often need multiple classes that implement the same interface. Often the initial decision is to have the classes inherit from a base class.

Inheritance can be used for providing a common interface for polymorphic behavior as well as for sharing common code. However, inheritance couples the base classes to the derived classes. You need to be sure that changes to the shared code do not adversely affect the behavior of the derived classes. To avoid this, you can provide a common interface, but follow the Gang of Four recommendation that states "Favor delegation over inheritance."

Create an interface, and have the classes implement that interface. If you find yourself starting to copy and paste the code from one implementing class into another, stop. Create a helper class, and extract the code into a method in that class. Delegate the behavior to the helper class. The following is an example:

```
interface CustomerLookup {
  Customer getCustomerByID(ID anID);
  Customer getCustomerByName(String name);
}
class MyCustomerLookup implements CustomerLookup {
  Customer getCustomerByName(String name){
    if (CustomerLookupHelper.checkValidName(name))
    // Do lookup
  }
}
class YourCustomerLookup implements CustomerLookup {
  Customer getCustomerByName(String name) {
    if (CustomerLookupHelper.checkValidName (name))
    // Do lookup
  }
}
class CustomerLookupHelper {
  static boolean checkValidName (String name) {
    // Do check
```

```
    }
}
```

MyCustomerLookup and YourCustomerLookup are related by the fact they perform the same behavior as designated by the Customer-Lookup interface. That they use common code (checkValidName) is little reason to have them inherit from the same class. The following is what it might look like if you use inheritance.

```
class CustomerLookup {
  abstract Customer getCustomerByID(ID anID);
  abstract Customer getCustomerByName(String name);
  boolean checkValidName (String name) {
    // Do check
  }
class MyCustomerLookup extends CustomerLookup {
  Customer getCustomerByName(String name){
    if (checkValidName(name))
      // Do lookup
  }
}
class YourCustomerLookup extends CustomerLookup {
  Customer getCustomerByName(String name) {
    if (checkValidName (name))
      // Do lookup
  }
}
```

The code is only a small amount shorter by eliminating the reference to the helper class. But the fact MyCustomerLookup and Your-CustomerLookup are derived from the same class can imply that there is more of a common implementation. Later on you may find that YourCustomerLookup and some new lookup, such as YourVendor-Lookup, have much more in common than YourCustomerLookup and MyCustomerLookup. If you avoid establishing an initial hierarchy, you can let your design emerge when you have determined the relevant relationships between types of CustomerLookups. This practice follows the lean principle of deferring commitment. Otherwise, you may wind up having to undo one hierarchy before creating a more relevant one.

Interfaces and Abstract Classes

Often there is a question as to the differences between an interface and an abstract class. From the language aspect, some languages that support the interface concept such as Java and C# allow a class to inherit from only one base class. If you use an abstract class to define the interface (for example, the methods and signature), then the derived classes will use up that one inheritance opportunity to achieve polymorphism. However, you can share any common implementation by making it part of the abstract class. Instead, if you have an interface, then the classes implementing it are still polymorphic, but you have not committed to using up the one chance for inheritance. However, if you have common methods, the implementations need to delegate that to a helper class, as previously shown, to avoid code duplication.

Interfaces and abstract classes both represent commonality of specification. Abstract classes also include commonality of implementation. This commonality can include both data attributes and methods. So, abstract classes couple the specification perspective and the implementation perspective.

It's possible you may find that as your code evolves, you have multiple implementations of an interface where each uses the same helper class to which they delegate. In that case, you might create an abstract class that implements the interface and that contains these helper functions. When the redundancy of always delegating to a helper class outweighs the effects of the coupling, then the change is justified. This is an example of emergent design.

Abstract classes are often used in frameworks and libraries but usually in the context of a well-examined area, such as graphic user interfaces and input/output. The design issues have already emerged.

Dependency Inversion Principle

Using interfaces makes your program conform to the Dependency Inversion principle.[12] This principle states that upper-level modules should not depend on lower-level modules. Both should depend upon abstractions. The interfaces represent these abstractions. In addition, abstractions should not depend upon the details; the details should depend upon the abstractions. Since an interface contains no implementation information, the details of the implementation cannot depend upon it. It is coupled only to the abstraction that the interface represents.

---

12. See www.objectmentor.com/resources/articles/dip.pdf.

Polymorphism in General

You do not need to use language constructs such as "interface" and "implements" to achieve polymorphism. Polymorphism is not in the form but in the intent. The term implies "multiple bodies" that provide the same behavior. For example, simply connecting to a different server that provides the same web service is employing polymorphism.

You can employ polymorphism at other times in the development cycle. For example, you could have two different source files that contained the same class that was implemented in two different ways. The following is an example.

```
// Desired Interface:

CustomerLookup {
  Customer getCustomerByID(ID anID);
}

// Source File: MyCustomerLookup

class CustomerLookup {
  Customer getCustomerByID(ID anID){
    // my code
  }
}
// Source File: YourCustomerLookup

class CustomerLookup {
  Customer getCustomerByID(ID anID) {
    // your code
  }
}
```

You compile them in separate modules. At load time or link time, you select which module to use. You get polymorphic behavior without involving a language construct.[13] This may be particularly useful if you are trying to mock a module that you do not have control over, so you cannot introduce interfaces into the module.

Using the UML syntax for an interface and implementing that interface clarifies that the polymorphism may be manifested in ways other than language constructs. As shown in Figure 6.1, the attribute <<interface>> denotes an interface, and a dashed line with a triangle indicates that the class implements that interface.[14]

---

13. In some languages such as C# and C++, you could place both versions into a single source file and use conditional compilation to select which one to use at compile time.
14. There is also a UML "lollipop" version of interfaces.

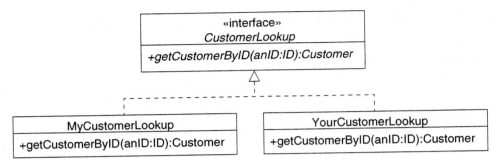

Figure 6.1   Class implementing interface

Not for Every Class

You don't have to have a separate interface declaration for every class. You simply have to think in those terms. Languages such as Java and C# mix implementation with the interface, as opposed to C++, which has a separate header file that allows for separation between interface and implementation. You can use the automatic documentation programs to create an interface description in Java and C# (the set of methods and their signatures). The operations should be understandable from the names on the documentation (Programming by Intention).

Summary

"Design to interfaces, not implementations," as the Gang of Four suggests. This ensures a separation of the specification perspective from the implementation perspective. This separation creates code that is easier to maintain. Apply tests to every interface to ensure that its implementation fulfills its contract including its protocol. Use test doubles or mocks to provide implementations of interfaces for testing purposes. "Favor delegation over inheritance" to avoid premature hierarchies and let your design emerge. Avoid coupling of specification and implementation perspectives by implementing interfaces rather than inheriting from an abstract class. An interface represents an abstract data type. Using abstract types creates more readable code.

CHAPTER 7

Acceptance Test–Driven Development (ATDD)

Acceptance tests ensure that a software system meets the requirements of a customer. Developing acceptance tests before starting to implement minimizes delays in development and the chances for miscommunication and misunderstanding. ATDD is as much the conversations about the tests as it is the tests themselves. These conversations are used to create common understanding of the requirements.[1]

Two Flows for Development

Building software requires people with three different focuses to collaborate: customers, developers, and testers. The customer facet (often represented by the "product owner" or "business analyst") determines the requirements, develops acceptance tests, and sets priorities. The developer centers on implementing the requirements and ensuring the implementation meets the acceptance tests. The tester focuses on helping the customer and developer to create acceptance tests and to pass those tests. Customer, developer, and tester focus often relates to titles. But in many agile shops, anyone on the team may take on these roles. This chapter describes some approaches you can employ in this three-way collaboration between the roles, regardless of titles.

Figure 7.1 shows a fairly traditional software-development process. It starts with a customer role eliciting a requirement and then analyzing it to see whether it is consistent and understandable. Based on the analysis, the developers create a design to describe how to implement the requirement. Next, they write the software code to implement the

---

1. Pugh, Ken. *Lean-Agile Acceptance Test–Driven Development: Better Software Through Collaboration.* Boston, MA: Addison-Wesley, 2011.

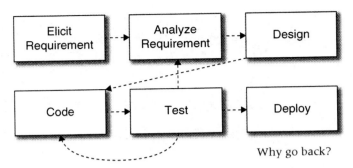

Figure 7.1 A traditional software development process

design and turn the executable code over to testers. The testers read the requirement and then create some functional tests that will verify that the program meets the requirement or needs further work. When the program finally meets the expected results and passes other tests, such as performance and usability tests, it is ready to be deployed.

In a perfect world, the system would pass through these stages in a linear fashion, one to the next. But perfection occurs only in fairy tales. In the real world of software development, there are misunderstandings that require loopbacks to correct—lots of misunderstandings! That distance between what you said and what we heard is very great indeed. When you said, "always," did you really mean "usually"? Did you mean to leave out the case when the user answers "no," or was that just an oversight? You failed to mention that the software would have to work at 98 percent reliability, across three continents, on and on. We humans are very good at not communicating very well.

Errors happen. And when they do, they must be corrected. But what was the error? Was it an error in implementation, or was it an error rising from an unclear requirement? Did the coder simply make a mistake? Did the customer forget to mention something?

That is why there are loopback lines in Figure 7.1. The tester informs the developer about an issue discovered in the code, and the developer must correct it. Or the tester and developer might end up revisiting the requirement to see whether there was a problem in interpretation, and that requires a loopback to the customer. Or after the customer has seen the system, something requires a change. Or there could even be a problem with the test itself. It is complicated and messy!

This cycling between the people playing the roles of tester, developer, and customer causes delay in deploying the product. And that adds to the cost of the product. Even worse, it can result in functionality being added to the code that is not needed, and that makes the system just that much more complex to maintain because it is rarely ever removed.

In his book *FIT for Developing Software*, Rick Mugridge makes the case for describing requirements in the form of tests. The process of defining the tests helps developers and testers validate their understanding of the requirements and helps customers assess whether what they are asking for is really what they want. It results in much greater clarity than merely asking lots of questions. The problem with asking questions is you are never sure that you have asked enough questions or even the right ones. It is the question that we don't *know* to ask that ends up causing us the most problems!

It is much better to use a process that results in quick feedback and clearer understanding. Figure 7.2 shows an alternative. As requirements are elicited, testers, developers, and the customer work out acceptance tests for the requirements.[2] These are specific examples of the requirement in action. The developer uses these tests when coding to ensure that the implementation meets the tests. When it does, the developer turns it over to the tester for the other types of tests, such as exploratory and usability testing.

The tests provide a center for collaboration between customer, developer, and tester that stands a better chance of understanding what the customer needs and what is required by the software to meet that need. The tests guarantee that the system does what the three parties wanted it to do.

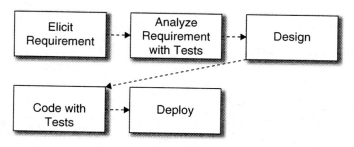

Figure 7.2   Acceptance Test–Driven Development flow

---

2. Sometimes customers have limited availability. In that case, the developer and tester may develop the acceptance tests and then validate them with the customer.

Acceptance Tests

Acceptance tests and requirements are linked. You can't have one without the other. The tests clarify and amplify the requirements.[3] A test that fails shows that the system does not properly implement a requirement. A test that passes is a specification of how the system works.

Acceptance tests as described in this chapter are not the traditional user acceptance tests, which are performed after implementation "by the end user to determine if the system is working according to the specification in the contract."[4] They are also not system tests that are usually independently written by testers by reading the requirements to ensure that the system meets those requirements.[5] However, all three types of tests are related in that they are all black-box tests; that is, they are independent of the implementation.

An Example Test

A customer role presents to the developer and tester roles a business rule for giving discounts. The stakeholder who created the rule wants to give discounts to the firm's customers. The discount will vary based on the type of customer.

The following is the business rule.[6]

> If Customer Type is **Good** and the Item Total is less than or equal $10,
>
> Then do not give a discount,
>
> Otherwise, give a 1 percent discount.
>
> If Customer Type is **Excellent**,
>
> Then give a discount of 1 percent for any order.
>
> If the Item Total is greater than $50,
>
> Then give a discount of 5 percent.

---

3. See Martin, Robert C., and Grigori Melnik. "Tests and Requirements, Requirements and Tests: A Möbius Strip." IEEE_Software Vol. 25, No. 1. January/February 2008 (http://www.gmelnik.com/papers/IEEE_Software_Moebius_GMelnik_RMartin.pdf).
4. See http://www.answers.com/topic/acceptance-test.
5. See http://www.answers.com/topic/system-test.
6. The rule is deliberately ambiguous for pedagogical purposes.

What is the discount for a customer who is Good and who has an order total greater than $50? What if the developer interpreted the rule to mean 1 percent and the tester interpreted the rule to mean 5 percent? Then there would be a defect that would need to be corrected. On the other hand, what if they both interpreted the rule to mean 5 percent? There might still be a defect, but it might escape into production and cost the company money in excessive discounts. And suppose they thought that *both* rules applied. It would cost even more!

A set of example calculations can clear up things. Table 7.1 shows examples of what the discount percentage should be for various values of Item Total and Discount Rating.

The first two rows show that the limit between giving a Good customer a discount or a 1 percent discount is $10. The "less than or equal" in the business rule is pretty clear. These two cases ensure that the implementation produced exactly that result. The third case shows that the interpretation was 1 percent for a Good customer with an Item Total greater than $50. The fourth example shows that the discount for an Excellent customer starts at the smallest possible Item Total. The fifth and sixth entries test that the discount increases just after the $50 point.

The customer was quite relieved when he worked through this table. Indeed, he did not want to give a 5 percent discount to Good customers!

Table 7.1   Examples of Discount Percentages

Item Total	Customer Rating	Discount Percentage
10.00	Good	0
10.01	Good	1
50.01	Good	1
.01	Excellent	1
50.00	Excellent	1
50.01	Excellent	5

Implementing the Acceptance Tests

There are at least four common ways to test the implementation.

- The tester role could create a test script that operates at the user interface level.

- The developer role could create a test user interface that allows checking the appropriate discount percentages.

- The tests could be performed with a unit testing framework.

- The tests could be implemented with an acceptance test framework.

User Interface Test Script

Suppose the program has a user interface that allows a customer to enter an order. The flow through the program is much like any application that processes orders. The user enters an order, and a summary screen appears, such as that shown in Figure 7.3.

The tester role creates a script to test each of the six examples. The tests might involve computing what the actual discount should be for each case. Unless the order summary screen shows this percentage, this is the only output that can be checked to make sure the calculation is correct.

Table 7.2 adds additional columns for the table that show the discount amount that should be applied.

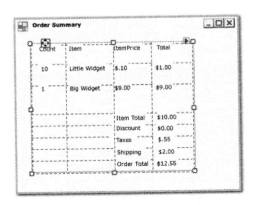

Figure 7.3   Acceptance test through the user interface

Table 7.2   Additional Examples of Discount Percentages

Item Total	Customer Rating	Discount Percentage	Discount Amount
10.00	Good	0	0.00
10.01	Good	1	0.10
50.01	Good	1	0.50
.01	Excellent	1	0.00
50.00	Excellent	1	0.50
50.01	Excellent	5	2.50

The script would go something like this:

1. Log on as a Customer who has the Rating listed in the table.

2. Start an order and put items in it until the total is the specified amount in the Item Total column on the test.

3. Check that the discount on the Order Summary screen matches the Discount Amount in the table.

4. The test would be repeated five more times for all six cases.

User Interface for Testing

To simplify the testing, the developer could create a user interface that is connected to the discount calculation module in the code. Although this interface would be used only during testing, it would cut down on the work required to show that the percentage was correctly determined. The user interface could be either a command-line interface or a graphical user interface. The graphical user interface might look like Figure 7.4.

With this user interface, a tester could enter all the combinations that are shown in the test table. The command-line interface might look like the following:

```
RunDiscountCalculatorTests <item_total>  <customer_type>
```

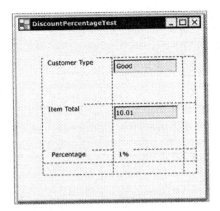

Figure 7.4   Acceptance test through the user interface

When it is run for a case, such as

```
RunDiscountCalculatorTests 10.00   Good
```

it would output the following result:

```
0
```

What these additional interfaces do is penetrate the normal user interface. The Order Summary screen connects to the system through the standard user interface layer. The Discount Percentage screen or `RunDiscountCalculatorTests` connects to some module inside the system, as shown in Figure 7.5. Let's call that module the Discount Calculator. By having a connection to the inside, a tester can check whether the internal behavior by itself is correct.

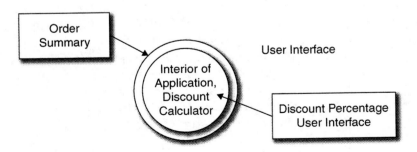

Figure 7.5   Acceptance test through the user interface

XUnit Testing

Another way is to use a unit testing framework to implement the tests for the discount calculator. The following is a sample of what these tests look like in the JUnit test framework.

```
class DiscountCalculatorTest {
  @Test
  public void testDiscountPercentageForCustomer() {
  DiscountCalculator dc = new DiscountCalculator();
    assertEquals(0, dc.computeDiscountPercentage(10.0,
      Customer.Good));
    assertEquals(1, dc.computeDiscountPercentage (10.01,
      Customer.Good));
    assertEquals(1, dc.computeDiscountPercentage (50.01,
      Customer.Good));
    assertEquals(1, dc.computeDiscountPercentage(.01,
      Customer.Excellent));
    assertEquals(1, dc.computeDiscountPercentage(50.0,
      Customer.Excellent));
    assertEquals(5, dc.computeDiscountPercentage(50.01,
      Customer.Excellent));
  }
}
```

Acceptance Test Framework

It is possible to automate a table such as this to execute the tests. Several test frameworks, such as Cucumber, Slim, and Robot Framework, allow you to describe tests with a table similar to the original table. Table 7.3 shows an example using FIT.[7]

When the test is run, FIT executes code that connects to the Discount Calculator. It gives the Discount Calculator the values in Item Total and Customer Rating. The Discount Calculator returns the Discount Percentage. FIT compares the returned value to the value in the table. If it agrees, the column shows up in green. If it does not, it shows up as red. You can't see the colors in black-and-white, so light gray represents green, and dark gray represents red. Table 7.4 shows that the implementation did not calculate the percentage correctly in the one case.

---

7. FIT was developed by Ward Cunningham. See http:// fit.c2.com, as well as Mugridge, R. and W. Cunningham. *Fit for Developing Software: Framework for Integrated Tests.* Upper Saddle River, NJ: Prentice Hall, 2005.

Table 7.3   FIT `fixture.Discount` Example

Item Total	Customer Rating	Discount Percentage()
10.00	Good	0
10.01	Good	1
50.01	Good	1
.01	Excellent	1
50.00	Excellent	1
50.01	Excellent	5

Table 7.4   FIT `fixture.Discount` Example

Item Total	Customer Rating	Discount Percentage()
10.00	Good	0
10.01	Good	1
50.01	Good	Expected 1, Actual 5
.01	Excellent	1
50.00	Excellent	1
50.01	Excellent	5

Connection

In the last three test forms, the order interface is not tested. The original script (User Interface Test Script) for the order interface should be run to make sure that the user interface is properly connected to the discount

Table 7.5   Discount Example

Item Total	Customer Rating	Discount Percentage	Discount Amount
10.01	Good	1	0.10
50.01	Excellent	5	2.50

percentage module. But unless there was a large risk factor involved, you might just run the script for a few cases such as that shown in Table 7.5.

An Exercise

In most of our classes we have people do an exercise to reflect on what happens when they don't write tests up front. It's worth the 5 to 10 minutes it'll take you to do this on your own. Doing the exercise is considerably different than thinking about doing the exercise. Do it on your own or with another co-worker.

1. Consider a time when you or your team wrote code without getting specific answers to the question "How will I know I've done that?" (referring to what has been asked of you) and where the customer later said, "That's not what I meant."

2. Now, consider what you think may have happened had you asked that question.

3. Repeat once or twice for full effect.

Our experience is that most people who don't ask the question "How will I know I've done that?" in response to a requirement usually have significant misunderstandings about the requirement.

What to Do If the Customer Won't Tell You

We often hear the lament that "Our customers won't talk to us to answer the question 'How will we know we've done that?'" Although this may be true, it doesn't lower the impact of proceeding without getting that question answered. Our suggestion is to figure out the answers yourself and then validate them with the customer. This isn't as good, but it accomplishes more or less the same need. Customers will often agree to review a set of answers that they wouldn't commit to coming up with themselves because it takes considerably less time to review than to create. Our recommendation is to never proceed without getting this question answered.

Summary

Acceptance Test–Driven Development is collaborating and improving our understanding through the development of acceptance tests. By having these conversations up front, we save a lot of rework later. Acceptance tests clarify understanding because they require both concepts (the requirement) and examples (the test specification). By actually implementing the test, we ensure our understanding as well increase our efficiency.

Tests for business logic can be executed in many ways.

- Creation through the user interface of a transaction that invokes the business rule

- Developing a user interface that invokes the business rule directly

- A test implemented in a language's unit testing framework

- An automated test that communicates to the business rule module

Our experience has shown that ATDD is perhaps the most impactful practice that development teams can do. Much of the value is in the conversations and definitions of the tests—something that all teams do. Hence, we strongly recommend it as a practice to adopt as early as possible. The added cost is not much since it's more about when you do your work, rather than adding new work.

PART II

General Attitudes

CHAPTER 8

Avoid Over- and Under-Design

Developers tend to take one of two approaches to programming. Many think they need to plan ahead to ensure that their system can handle new requirements that come their way. Unfortunately, this planning ahead often involves adding code to handle situations that never come up. The end result is code that is more complex than it needs to be and therefore harder to change—the exact situation they were trying to avoid. The alternative, of course, seems equally bad. That is, they just jump in, code with no forethought, and hope for the best. But this hacking also typically results in code that is hard to modify. What are we supposed to do that doesn't cause extra complexity but leaves our code easy to change? The middle ground can be summed up by something Ward Cunningham said at a user group: "Take as much time as you need to make your code quality as high as it can be, but don't spend a second adding functionality that you don't need now!" In other words, write high-quality code, but don't write extra code.

This chapter is admittedly more of a new mantra than it is a detailed description of a technique to implement. This chapter takes advantage of what we learned in Chapter 5, Encapsulate That!, and sets the groundwork for Chapter 11, Refactor to the Open-Closed.

A Mantra for Development

We believe developers should have a particular attitude when writing code. There are actually several we've come up with over time—all being somewhat consistent with each other but saying things a different way. The following are the ones we've held to date:

- Avoid over- and under-design.

- Minimize complexity and rework.

- Never make your code worse (the Hippocratic Oath of coding).

- Only degrade your code intentionally.

- Keep your code easy to change, robust, and safe to change.

Before we can discuss these mantras, we need to be clear what we mean by quality code. Appendix B, Code Qualities, provides a thorough explanation of the specific qualities referred to in this chapter. We'll give a brief summary of code quality here, but interested readers may want to read the more extensive narrative in the appendix.

The Pathologies of Code Qualities

It's often easier to see code qualities by discussing examples of when the qualities aren't present. Let's look at five common code qualities: cohesion, coupling, redundancy, readability, and encapsulation.

- **Cohesion.** Strongly cohesive classes are classes whose functions are all related to each other. Strongly cohesive methods are methods that do only one thing. The pathology of weak cohesion is classes or methods that do unrelated things. We've heard very weakly cohesive classes called "god objects" presumably because they are somewhat omniscient in that everything takes place in them.[1]

- **Proper coupling.** Having well-defined relationships between objects makes them easier to understand and likely to inadvertently cause problems when changing code. The pathology of improper coupling is the occurrence of side effects—that is, unexpected errors due to making changes elsewhere.

- **No redundancy.** No redundancy is difficult to achieve. The more redundancy you have, the more time it will take to make changes. As we discussed in Chapter 4, Shalloway's Law and Shalloway's Principle, no redundancy is virtually impossible to achieve—but at least you want to make it so you don't have to find the duplication. Essentially, the pathology of redundancy is that when you make a change in one place, you have to make a change in another place.

---

1. We've also thought they may be called this because when you first look at them you mutter to yourself "Oh my god!" and the fact that it looks like only god could figure them out.

- **Readability.** Readable code means you can understand what has been written. It requires intention-revealing names and is best achieved by using Programming by Intention (see Chapter 1, Programming by Intention). Unreadable code, of course, is code you can't understand when you read it. Poor names, tight coupling, and big methods/classes contribute greatly to the unreadability of code.

- **Encapsulation.** Encapsulation is more than mere data hiding. The type of an object is one of the most important things to hide. Design patterns are really about hiding: object type, cardinality, which function is being used, order, optional behavior, construction, and more. The pathology of encapsulation is when you must know how the code you are using is implanted in order to use it properly. This often means you know the implementation type of the object being used or know something about cardinality, order, and so on.

Avoid Over- and Under-Design

This essentially means you should put in the correct amount of design. Overdesign is putting in things that add complexity to the code that may or may not be needed. Note that the key word here is "complexity." We're not as worried about the time you take as much as we are about how you leave the state of the code. If the work you've done does not raise the complexity of the code you have, then no worries. In other words, putting in an interface where one may or may not be needed is not necessarily a bad thing if everyone understands interfaces. Interfaces aren't really complexity-adders in our mind. They are a holder for an idea. However, putting in a complex parameter list (or using a value object to hold a parameter, say, when one isn't needed) would be raising complexity.

Under-design is actually a euphemism for "poor code quality." We view under-design as having taken place when high coupling or weak cohesion is present. Typically, proper encapsulation is also not present. So, avoiding overdesign means make your code changeable, but don't add things you don't need now. If you need them later, the changeability of the code will enable you to do that with less, if any, extra cost. Avoiding under-design mostly means making sure your code is changeable.

Minimize Complexity and Rework

Many people only partly understand the true nature of refactoring. Martin Fowler, in his excellent *Refactoring: Improving the Design of Existing Code*,[2] describes refactoring in the following way.

> *Refactoring is the process of changing a software system in such a way that it does not alter the external behavior of the code yet improves its internal structure. It is a disciplined way to clean up code that minimizes the chances of introducing bugs. In essence when you refactor you are improving the design of the code after it has been written.*

In the book, Fowler talks about refactoring as a method of cleaning up messy/poor code. However, there is another side to refactoring that Fowler doesn't talk about. This is refactoring code that is of high quality, when it comes to the code qualities we've been talking about, but that no longer has sufficient design because of new requirements. In other words, the book talks about how to clean up poorly written code (a good thing to know) but mostly ignores how to refactor good code that now must be changed to accommodate new requirements.[3]

We strongly suggest that refactoring good code when new requirements come so that the code is better able to accommodate the changes is a way to minimize complexity because you are deferring adding complexity until it is needed, but your code quality is high so there is no rework. We would contend that delaying extensions to code is not rework but a kind of just-in-time design. We'll talk explicitly about how to do this in Chapter 11, Refactor to the Open-Closed.

Never Make Your Code Worse/Only Degrade Your Code Intentionally

Existing code degrades one bit at a time (no pun intended). We suggest that team members do their best to not take shortcuts that makes their code worse. Sometimes this is difficult, however. It may be that legacy code makes it very difficult to add functionality properly without harming your code. To be realistic, we restate "Never make your code worse"

---

2. Fowler, Martin. *Refactoring: Improving the Design of Existing Code*. Boston, MA: Addison-Wesley, 1999.
3. Alan Shalloway had a private conversation with Martin about this once. After suggesting that the refactoring concepts Martin presented would work equally well for both types of code, Martin responded by agreeing and saying, "My book was long enough as it was!"

to "Only degrade your code intentionally." Although this may sound funny, the alternative would be to make your code worse *unintentionally*.

One way to only degrade your code intentionally is to ensure you consider alternatives. One way to do this is to make a teamwide agreement that if developers can't figure out how to make a change without degrading code, they will tell another team member of the change they are thinking of making before they make the change. Note that we are not requiring getting permission or even getting a better result. We're just suggesting you tell someone. This forces you to at least reflect a little. Our experience has shown us that a person will stop just short of a good solution because he or she is willing to do the first thing that comes to mind. Our approach forces people to think about things a bit more (sometimes a lot more because they don't want to admit to coworkers that they don't have good solutions).

Keep Your Code Easy to Change, Robust, and Safe to Change

Code should not be viscous. That means the effort to make changes should not be excessive. Viscosity can be avoided by having easy-to-understand, nonredundant code. Code should also not be brittle. That is, changes in one place should not break code in other places. This requires loosely coupled code, following Shalloway's principle (see Chapter 4, Shalloway's Law and Shalloway's Principle) and proper encapsulation. It is not sufficient to follow these two mantras alone, however. Although doing so may make it easy to change your code with less likelihood of breaking it, there are no guarantees. The only way to be assured that you can safely change your code is to have a full set of automated acceptance tests available.

A Strategy for Writing Modifiable Code in a Non-Object-Oriented or Legacy System

Many of the approaches we've discussed here are often met with this attitude: "That's a great idea, but I can't do it where I work because I'm using C." A variant of this is "That's a great idea, but I can't do it where I work because there is so much monolithic legacy code that I can't take advantage of object-oriented methods." There are other variants as well, but you get the idea. Although it is true that your existing software and the languages you are using provide certain constraints on what you can do, there are certain approaches you can *always* take. One of these is to consider the separation of concerns in a different way.

The idea is to separate the code that is particular to the application from the code that defines the application's architecture (or even system architecture).

One can think of a program as essentially an overall flow detailing the steps to be undertaken. For example, a sales-order system can have a variety of actions needed to work:

- Select customer.

- Get customer information.

- Select products to be sold.

- Get prices.

- Apply appropriate discounts.

- Total cost of sales order.

- Specify shipping.

Object orientation attempts to simplify this by creating objects that group responsibilities for the different implementing steps. These objects collaborate with each other and avoid coupling by having well-defined interfaces that hide their implementations. Unfortunately, if you can't (properly) use an object-oriented language, how can you get at least some of the value that comes from separating concerns? One way is to have each method in your code deal with only one of the following:

- The system architecture

- The application architecture

- The implementation of a step

For example, let's say you are writing embedded software that takes its input from a special bus in the form of string from which it extracts required parameters via a specialized method. Applications like this often take the following approach:

```
public function someAction () {
  string inputString;
```

```
inputString= getInputFromBus();
  if (getParameter(inputString, PARAM1)> SOMEVALUE) {
    // bunches of code
  } else {
    if (getParameter(inputString, PARAM2)< SOMEOTHERVALUE) {
      // more bunches of code
      // ...
    } else {
      // even more bunches of code
      // ...
    }
  }
}
```

The problem with this is lack of cohesion. As you try to figure out what the code does, you are also confronted with detailed specifics about how the information is obtained. Although this might be clear to the person who first wrote this, this will be difficult to change in the future (not counting the confusion that happens now). This gets much worse if one never makes the distinction between the system one is embedded in (which is determining the input method) and the logic inside the routine. For example, consider what happens when a different method of getting the string is used as well as a different method of extracting the information. In this case, the parameters are returned in an array:

```
public function someAction () {
  string inputString;
  int values[MAX_VALUES];

  if (COMMUNICATION_TYPE== TYPE1) {
    inputString= getInputFromBus();
  } else {
    values= getValues();
  }

  if ( (COMMUNICATION_TYPE== TYPE1 ?
    getParameter( inputString, PARAM1) :
    values[PARAMETER1]) > SOMEVALUE) {
    // bunches of code
  } else {
    if ( COMMUNICATIONS_TYPE== TYPE1 ?
      getParameter( inputString, PARAM2) :
      values(PARAMETER2])
      < SOMEOTHERVALUE) {
      // more bunches of code
      // ...
```

```
  } else {
    // even more bunches of code
    // …
  }
 }
}
```

Pretty confusing? Well, have no fears, it'll only get worse. If, instead, we separated the "getting of the values" from the "using of the values," things would be much clearer.

```
public function someAction () {
  string inputString;
  int values[MAX_VALUES];

  int value1;
  int value2;

  if (COMMUNICATION_TYPE== TYPE1) {
    inputString= getInputFromBus();
  } else {
    values= getValues();
  }

  value1= (COMMUNICATION_TYPE== TYPE1 ?
    getParameter( inputString, PARAM1) :
    values[PARAMETER1]);
  value2= ( COMMUNICATIONS_TYPE== TYPE1 ?
    getParameter( inputString, PARAM2) :
    values(PARAMETER2]);

  someAction2( value1, value2);
}

public function someAction2 (int value1, int value2) {

  if ( value1 > SOMEVALUE) {
    // bunches of code
  } else {
    if ( value2 < SOMEOTHERVALUE) {
      // more bunches of code
      // …
    } else {
      // even more bunches of code
      // …
    }
  }
}
```

You must remember that complexity is usually the result of an increase in the communication between the concepts involved, not the concepts themselves. Therefore, complexity can be lowered by separating different aspects of the code. This does not require object orientation. It simply requires putting things in different methods.

Summary

Developers must always be aware of doing too much or too little. When you anticipate what is needed and put in functionality to handle it, you are very likely to be adding complexity that may not be needed. If you don't pay attention to your code quality, however, you are setting yourself up for rework and problems later. Code quality is a guide. Design patterns can help you maintain it because they give you examples of how others have solved the problem in the past in similar situations.

CHAPTER 9

Continuous Integration

The creation of developer tools is often guided by the needs of developers as they are discovered over time. Tools, however, can have an influence on process, which in turn can create challenges for the very developers who asked for the tools in the first place. An example of this is version control. Version control has been widely adopted as a way of ensuring that code can be returned to a previous state when the team realizes it has gone down a bad path or when the customer decides against developing a given feature. Version control creates a feeling of "safety" but also brings along another concept, namely, source code branching. This chapter will examine the reasons for, and negative effects of, branching the code base, and how, through continuous integration (CI) and good design, we might eliminate the need for branching in the first place.

Branching the Source Code

Why do virtually all version control systems allow for the source code to be branched? By "branching," we mean the ability to fork off a specialized version of the source code, into its own storage space, to be worked on separately from the latest version of the code, often called the "trunk."

The addition of this capability came from development needs that can be categorized into two general cases.

- **Specialization branching.** The team needs to create a specialized version of the code for a given customer. They take the "generic" form of the code as a starting-off point and then modify, expand, scale up, add features, performance tune, and so on, all based on the needs of the given customer. They may do this repeatedly for various customers. These specialized branches will never be merged back into the main trunk, because they are appropriate only for the customers they were created for.

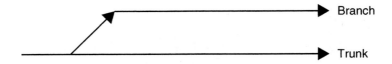

- **Development branching.** One developer or group of developers needs to be able to work on one part of the system without concern that the work of other developers will break their changes, or vice versa. In other words, they want to work in isolation for a while, in their own development sandbox. Eventually, the work they do will be "merged" back into the main trunk.

Multiple Versions: Specialization Branching

Specialization branching is better handled by improving the design of the system in order to make the key shared functionality more modular and thus reusable without having to create special versions of it. Design patterns, and good design in general, can make this much easier to achieve.

In a sense, when the team "specializes a branch," it is very much akin to using object inheritance to create specialized classes, with all the downfalls of this approach (see Chapter 13, When and How to Use Inheritance).

In Figure 9.1 we see a trunk with versions V_1, V_2, and V_3 specialized from it; V_{3a} is specialized from V_3. All five versions are maintained at all times.

This works, but it creates coupling and redundancies that can make maintenance very problematic in the future.

For example, when there are many specialized versions of a system, what happens when a bug is discovered? Each special version must be debugged on its own, even though the bug may be essentially the same in all cases. Similarly, what if there is a change that affects all these

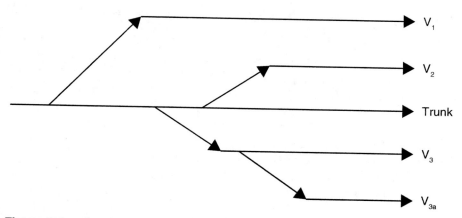

Figure 9.1   Specialization branches coexist indefinitely.

special versions? Here again, the effort needed to implement the change will have to be expended in each special case.

In good design, the main core capabilities are developed separately from the various subsystems that need them and are then reused through strongly encapsulating interfaces. Much of the rest of this book is about achieving just this quality of design.

For example, consider one capability of a banking system. At its core, it will likely have a mechanism for transferring funds from one account to another. This core capability will show up differently when we consider different needs.

- At the ATM, a given customer can use this capability but only for that customer's own accounts.

- At the teller workstation, the teller can transfer money from any account to any other account, but perhaps the amount is limited to a particular maximum.

- At the bank manager workstation, the manager can transfer any amount from any account to any other account.

- At the online banking website, the ATM functionality is made available through a web interface but obviously without the ability to deposit or withdraw.

Separating the needs of the clients as they are reflected by the system capabilities from their encapsulating the specific implementations removes the need for specialization branching. Even if we can achieve this, however, the second motivation for branching will still exist.

Working in Isolation: Development Branching

The fact that the actions of one developer or team can affect the work of another developer or team is a force driving the branching capabilities of version-control systems. In essence, we need to protect the integrity of the trunk and to prevent developers from interfering with each other's work. In essence, by branching we encapsulate our work. Even in systems with well-designed componentization, this can happen within a given component or by changes made to cross-component concerns (such as changes to the interfaces of core capabilities).

This encapsulation, however, must not last, and the safety provided by it of branching carries with it a potentially high cost: the need to merge the branch(es) back into the main trunk (see Figure 9.2) when we are done developing our new feature or making a given change.

It is the day most developers have come to dread: the code freeze and the merge. The only real winner on this day is the developer or team who *checks in first*. Everyone else is going to have to suffer with merging with an ever-diverging trunk.

The cost of the merging process is directly relative to the complexity of the merge. The complexity of the merge is determined by several factors, such as the following:

- The number of files involved

- The number of changes to each file

- The nature and scope of the changes, whether they are local or systemwide

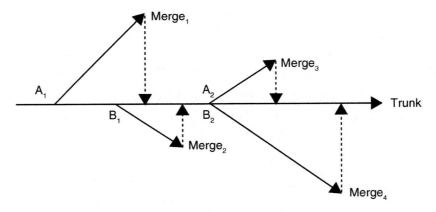

Figure 9.2   Development branches merged back into the trunk

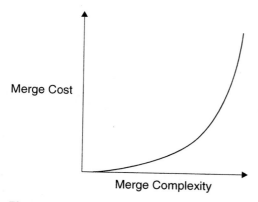

Figure 9.3   Complexity leads to increased cost.

   This relationship is not linear (see Figure 9.3). The more complex the merge is, the longer it will take and the more difficult it will be. This pain will not only be felt by the development team but also by the business that must pay the cost of delaying the introduction of this and subsequent features.

   Two related factors influence the amount of complexity surrounding any given merge: the time elapsed since the previous merge and the number (and size) of changes made in that time (that is, complexity) (see Figure 9.4). We can focus on time, of course, since in general we would expect changes made in a shorter time to be less numerous and smaller.

   The conclusion is straightforward: The longer we wait between merges, the more expensive the merge process will be (see Figure 9.5). By reducing the time between merges, we reduce the cost of change. If

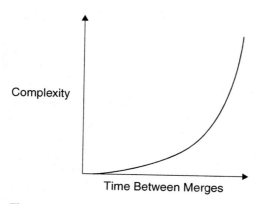

Figure 9.4   Having infrequent merges leads to increased complexity.

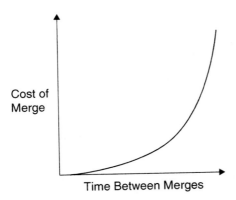

Figure 9.5   Having less frequent merges leads to increased cost.

the time is short enough, most merges can be handled automatically by automated tools.

We have the ability to influence the time between merges simply by dictating that we will merge more often, but here we fall into a common syndrome: A new solution we arrive at causes a new problem to be addressed.

Problem, Solution, Problem

Let's examine the chain of thought in this chapter thus far.

- **Problem.** We want to make sure that our work will not affect the existing functionality and others' work.

- **Solution.** We will branch the code and work on our own branch.

- **Problem.** But if we branch, we must merge, and merging is painful, especially if the time between merges is large.

- **Solution.** Make the time between merges small.

Now we have a new problem. Every time we merge the code, we have to ensure that the merge does not create instability in the system. This is the overhead that accompanies each and every merge and does not have to do with the complexity of the merge per se.

If we decide to commit more frequently, we will most likely reduce the complexity of the merge, but we will also increase the frequency of merging and thus increase the amount of time spent on the overhead that accompanies each merge.

The "Nightly Build"

Many teams employ the practice of a nightly build. Because it happens only at night, it is a relatively infrequent opportunity to merge and therefore carries a higher cost.

If the cost of verifying the entire system is high, it does not necessarily have to deter the team from engaging in continuous integration. If the system is well-componentized and each component is comprehensively tested on its own, then the team may decide that the risk of breaking another component is low enough to allow for a nightly build process to discover any intercomponent problems.

The Merge-Back

A question remains unanswered. What should the rest of the team do when someone else has merged their code into the trunk?

Two options are available:

- Ignore the new version of the code until it is their time to check in, in which case they need to merge their code with the new version (see Figure 9.6).

- Grab the latest version and integrate it with their work in progress, incorporating the latest changes into their code immediately.

Option 2 can appear a bit tedious when we note that every time someone checks their code into the system, a merge is mandated. If we

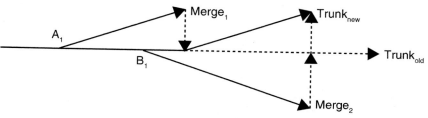

Figure 9.6   Ignoring another team's merge means you will have to incorporate their changes later.

do not do this, however, we end up with a second merge every time we commit.

If we decide to incorporate another team's change when it is committed, we call this a "merge-back" because it merges from the trunk back to your code (see Figure 9.7).

"I will never get any work done; I'll be constantly merging" may be your response.

The upside is that the code you're working on is always up-to-date, and any changes made by others present themselves as soon as they are done. This minimizes the risk of your code diverging from the current state of the trunk and hence the risk of rework. Also, keep in mind that if this is done frequently, the cost of merge becomes trivial and in most cases is done automatically when you get the latest version. In fact, any conflicts that ensue are things you have to address immediately because they indicate that your code has just become significantly different from the trunk.

Option 1 seems to solve the problem of constant merge-backs because there are none. You merge your code only before you check it in. But this presents us with the same problem we are trying to solve, which is the complexity of merging code after a long period of time.

This overhead increases as the time between merges increases, and not just because of the complexity of each merge. Let's say that we have a trunk version of the code, which we'll call A. I go off and start working on a branch "A with B added." You, at the same time, create your own branch "A with C added." I get done first, so I check my code in, requiring that I validate that my changes do not negatively affect the main version. You are still working on A with C added, but at some point you will have to incorporate B into what you are doing, because it may well affect A (which you are working with) or may mean you need to do something different with C than you originally thought.

Now consider the situation with three, four, or five different teams. Each team will have to consider this decision, and its impact, each

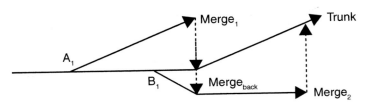

Figure 9.7   Merging back immediately

time another team commits their changes to the main trunk. If we can ensure that each team knows, as soon as possible, that a change needs to be incorporated into the work they are currently engaging, we can drastically reduce this cost.

Test-Driven Development and Merge Cost

Part of the cost of merging is verifying the correctness of the code after it has been merged. Properly coordinating the merge and merge-back ensures that the system will compile (there are no breaking changes) but not that it has the correct behavior as indicated by the requirements. That the behavior is still correct must be verified as well.

So, the cost of a merge is the merge itself, the merge-back, and the verification of each (see Figure 9.8).

If this verification requires developer effort, then reducing the time between merges (which increases the frequency of merging) may eventually create more cost than it saves. Most development teams realize this and seek out a sweet spot (see Figure 9.9): the balance between the size of the merge (too big, too expensive) and the number of merges in a given time frame (too many, too expensive).

$$\text{Cost of a single merge} = (\text{Merge} + \text{VerifyMerge} + \text{MergeBack} + \text{VerifyMergeBack})$$

$$\text{Cost of change} = \sum(\text{Merge} + \text{VerifyMerge} + \text{MergeBack} + \text{VerifyMergeBack})$$

$$= \sum(\text{Merge} + \text{MergeBack}) + \sum(\text{VerifyMerge} + \text{VerifyMergeBack})$$

TDD can fundamentally change this equation. We promote TDD in this book as a way of creating a verifiable functional specification of the

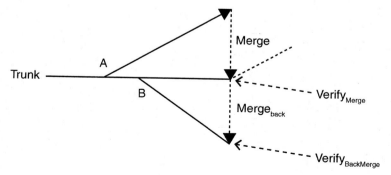

Figure 9.8   Merging, back-merging, and verification

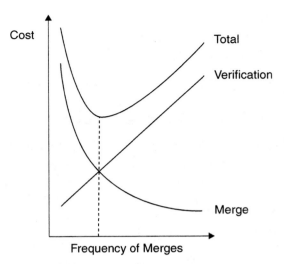

Figure 9.9   Attempting to reduce the total cost of changes, where the dashed line is the "sweet spot"

system, one that will not lose value over time. However, the value of TDD does not stop there. We note that it also provides the code coverage that makes refactoring less dangerous, and here we see that it also can reduce the overhead of merging (see Figure 9.10).

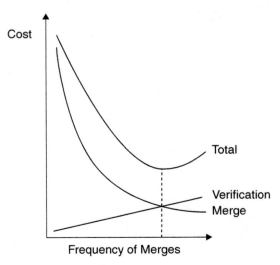

Figure 9.10   TDD reduces the cost of verification and therefore the total cost of change. How sweet it is!

With an automated test suite, we can reduce the cost of this verification to essentially zero, especially if the tests we write were done in the TDD style (that is, focused on specifying the proper behavior of the system).

In TDD we typically write tests first, allow them to fail, and then write the code that is needed to get them to pass. Thus, all code is written to turn some given red test into a green test, and as a result each piece of code is covered (by the very test it turned green). This code coverage can be used to verify the correctness of the code by simply running the tests as part of the merging process.

With the overhead of merging reduced, we can reexamine the balance between the merge's size and frequency and in so doing can minimize the total cost of change. You'll note that the cost of change can still rise if our merge frequency increases too much; integrating on every keystroke is not quite the best of ideas.

Continuous Integration

Continuous integration means that each time a change to the code has been completed, we immediately commit this change into the main trunk and inform everyone that this has happened so they can merge back.

In a well-factored system (with plenty of encapsulation and open-closedness), we expect that this will, under most circumstances, have no effect on other teams working on other aspects of the system.

Automated tests have two roles here:

- When the code turns a red test green, the change is "completed," and this should trigger an immediate commit. It essentially defines the notion of "complete."

- However, even if all code compiles after a change is committed, it is possible that one of the tests that another team has not yet checked in will start to fail. This is our indication that the *behavior* of the system has changed in such a way that the work of another team is now no longer correct; and the failing test, in this case, informs us quickly of this fact.

Naturally we want this process to be as efficient as possible, and to this end a number of tools have been created to automate the notification of committed changes across the team and the running of all tests when this happens. Regardless of the preferred tool, however, the process is essentially the same. Note that the size of the changes and therefore the costs remain low and consistent.

In continuous integration (see Figure 9.11), when you are ready to commit, you do the following:

- You get the latest version.

- You merge back any changes in it into your code.

- You check in the result (the version-control system ensures that you are working on the latest version or requires you to get the latest version and merge back again).

- Each merge must include running all tests, and if *any* of them break, it is the responsibility of the developer currently checking to correct the problem (even if it is not this developer's area).

Automated tools are crucial for the success of a continuous integration effort. We need to consider the source-control system and the build system.

The following are some required features of a source-control system that supports continuous integration.

- Does not require explicit checkouts but rather performs silent, automatic merges

- Ensures atomic commits—if one file fails to check in, all other files in the same check-in will be unaltered.

- Deals efficiently with small changes

- Has a notification mechanism when a check in succeeds—this is important to kick off the build process

- Tracks all changes through filename changes

An example of such a system is Subversion.

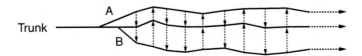

Figure 9.11   Continuous integration

Continuous Integration Servers

Many teams like to use continuous integration servers to reinforce the soundness and correctness of the build. The continuous integration server is responsible for triggering the build and postbuild activities when a change is detected in the source-control system.

At a minimum, it should be able to do the following:

- Detect changes to the source tree

- Kick off a build

- Run automated tests

- Report failures in either build or tests

- Report successful builds so that the team members can merge back the latest version

The following are examples of tools that work this way (stated in no particular order).

- CruiseControl (open source, via SourceForge)

- TeamCity (JetBrains)

- FinalBuilder (VSoft)

- Team Foundation Server (Microsoft)

- Cabie (open source, via Tigris.org)

Some systems actually run the build and then only if the build is successful (including tests) will check the code, on behalf of the developer, into the source-control system.

As good as the CI server concept is, it introduces a major bottleneck. The time it takes to go through a complete merge cycle on the CI server limits the merge frequency for the entire team. Several approaches can be taken to solve this problem.

- **Do not run a CI server.** During the workday, rely on the merge and validation done by the individual developers' machines, and delegate a complete system build and verification to a nightly build.

- **Start a CI server build only when it is idle.** This means that as the system is built and verified, multiple merges will occur on the trunk and will be tested when the current run completes. An alternative to this approach is to have the CI server work on a schedule, say, every half an hour, pursuant on a merge having occurred since the last build.

- **Beef up the CI server.** The CI server should be a powerful machine or a collection of machines capable of running multiple builds concurrently as well as distributing the execution of the tests in a single build. Running the tests in parallel is possible since good tests are independent of each other and running them in parallel can significantly reduce the CI server bottleneck.

Note that it is crucial for the developers' environments and the CI server environment to be identical. If you find that it is not, because the merge succeeds on the developer machine and fails on the CI server, steps must be taken to investigate and correct the causes for the failure.

Summary

Continuous integration is a crucial practice that can improve the development team's efficiency by doing the following:

- Reducing the time spent on merging changes into the main source tree.

- Improving intrateam communication by making the work done by the team members visible early. This gives the team a chance to observe and comment on changes done to the code base—both in content and in organization as soon as they occur.

- Limiting the impact of design changes as they take effect immediately after they are introduced. This allows quick integration of the changes into the work in progress as well as an early opportunity to discuss them in case disagreements arise within the team as to their correctness.

Every time a merge occurs, a cost is incurred. This cost is usually low but must still be kept in mind. Every merge requires a series of merge-backs by other team members as well as the verification that no existing functionality or work in progress is broken. Whereas the cost of the merge and merge-backs drops as the merge frequency (and hence size) drops, the cost of verification is usually a constant. This means you *can* merge too often.

Identifying the appropriate frequency of merge is crucial for a successful continuous integration practice. One way of attenuating these diminishing returns is to throttle the frequency of merge-backs to an acceptable level. The team members may decide to merge back every certain amount of time or after a set amount of merges has occurred rather than after each one.

TDD is very instrumental in reducing the verification time and raising the accuracy of the verification process. It also allows partial work to be merged because there is no risk in breaking the existing functionality or any of the partial functionality merged into the system. There are always tests to protect it.

Choosing a suitable source-control system is crucial for continuous integration to succeed. The system should be low ceremony, be atomic, and allow files to be worked on concurrently. It should have a powerful automatic merge capability and the notification mechanism to notify team members that a new version is available for merge-back.

The team may choose to use a CI server to further reinforce the soundness of the merges. This introduces a process bottleneck that will need to be resolved. The more developers who work on the system, the more restricting this bottleneck will be. Several strategies exist for dealing with this bottleneck.

PART III

Design Issues

CHAPTER 10

Commonality and Variability Analysis

Most people were taught to do object-oriented analysis and design by finding the nouns and verbs in their problem domain, converting the nouns to classes and the verbs to functions. Unfortunately, this approach does not work well in the real world. It inherently leads to tall class hierarchies or embedded switches/if statements.[1] When building software in an iterative manner, you must learn to create and organize objects in a different manner, around the concepts that are present in your problem domain. Design patterns offer examples for doing this. Commonality-Variability Analysis offers a straightforward way to find these concepts.

In this chapter, we explore a technique that will help you identify the entities in a problem domain and identify what they have in common in order to define their abstractions. We will see how to separate related abstractions from each other in order to create a more elegant model of our problem domain. We'll see how this model can guide our implementations. We will also illustrate a technique, or tool, called the Analysis Matrix[2] that can be used to facilitate the conversation between customers (or their proxies), designers/coders, and testers.

Using Nouns and Verbs as a Guide: Warning, Danger Ahead!

If object-oriented designs are supposed to reflect the problem domain, then defining objects from what we find in the problem domain seems to be a reasonable approach. The trouble is that being guided by what

---

1. This phenomenon is described in great detail in Shalloway and Trott's *Design Patterns Explained: A New Perspective on Object-Oriented Design, Second Edition.*
2. The Analysis Matrix was first described in *Design Patterns Explained: A New Perspective on Object-Oriented Design.*

you know about now is very specific. It does not prepare you for what you will have in the future. In fact, it can lock you in with assumptions about the domain—assumptions that aren't always verified and assumptions that, after they are made, make the code hard to change.

Here is an example: Suppose you are developing an application for a college. In this application, there is a class named Student. At some point, you discover you need to handle students from other countries. You decide to model these foreign students by creating a specialized class. Now, your application has a Student and a special kind of student: ForeignStudent. Later, the college decides to start a foreign-exchange program, so you add another special kind of ForeignStudent: ForeignExchangeStudent. And right there, you have built an unexamined assumption into your system. You have assumed that all foreign-exchange students are foreign, but that is not always the case. What about someone who had studied abroad and then decided to join the college's foreign-exchange program to study for one quarter because she was homesick? She isn't a foreign student, just a member of the Foreign Exchange Student Program. Now what? Before too long, you have an application with highly coupled objects and very tall class hierarchies.[3]

Your software must serve the real world, and the real world is more complex than what we assume.

Creating good, decoupled hierarchies is hard, especially when you have to create new variants of entities you have already modeled. And it is worse because you often have to add to several hierarchies simultaneously. It is even harder because these variations are often embedded into the context of their use. Although it looks like you just need to tweak the system a little, the reality is far different. It takes far more time to *integrate* new features than it does to write them in the first place.

Let's look at an example to see what the problem is, and then let's look for an alternative path.

Suppose you are writing the controller software for a disk drive and you currently have to support two drives:

- C4DD_XYZ: 4 heads, 20 tracks, encrypting Algorithm A

- C4DD_UVW: 2 heads, 40 tracks, encrypting Algorithm B

---

3. It is interesting to note that biologists have given up trying to create hierarchies of living things. Plants and animals have overlapping characteristics.

The different number of heads and tracks requires different algorithms for placing data on the drives themselves.

Using the "nouns and verbs" approach to design the classes, you might represent the two different disk drives by defining two different classes, named C4DD_XYZ and C4DD_UVW. At a minimum, you will have to come up with a set of methods that implement the needed behavior of these such as Read() and Write().

Since we are trying to be object-oriented, we notice that since both C4DD_XYZ and C4DD_UVW are controllers, they should have a common base class, as shown in Figure 10.1.

Now, suppose a new, faster model gets introduced. Model C4DD_UVW2 is like the original model C4DD_UVW. It has 2 heads and 40 tracks and uses Algorithm B for encryption just as the others do; however, because it is a faster drive, its tracking algorithm needs to change. We might insert an if statement in the code to specify which tracking algorithm to use based on which model is currently installed. Or, taking a more object-oriented approach, we might create a C4DD_UVW base class and then extend two classes from it: C4DD_UVW1 (the original model) and C4DD_UVW2 (the new model), as shown in Figure 10.2.

So far, so good. Extending classes in this way does work, at least for now; however, with more and more models, this approach will break down. For example, what if a few of the specialized classes need to use the same service? If you have been very disciplined and if you have been doing Programming by Intention (see Chapter 1, Programming by Intention), you might be able to refactor your code and move the service up a level. But accounting for the exceptions might make it hard. We created this problem for ourselves when we started down the path of specialization by refining nouns. Or consider what happens if there is a third variation of C4DD_UVW that needs to use Algorithm A, the encryption algorithm from C4DD_XYZ. The right thing might be to extract Algorithm A from C4DD_XYZ, but you don't have time: Someone else wrote C4DD_XYZ, and maybe extracting Algorithm A would mean

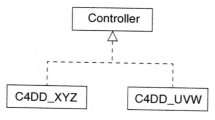

Figure 10.1   The controllers

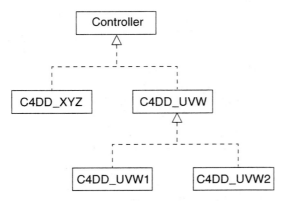

Figure 10.2   UML model describing the new design .

having to retest the C4DD_XYZ code. If the team that wrote it is unwilling to do that, it may not be feasible to break out the algorithm. What should you do? It is tempting just to copy Algorithm A from C4DD_XYZ and then paste it into the new C4DD_UVW3. It is tempting, but it would be wrong. Inevitably, there will come a need to change Algorithm A. Then you are stuck having to find every place you have done the copy and paste. Heaven help you if you miss one! And Shalloway's law[4] guarantees you will.

What Is the Real Problem?

In this example, the problem is not using inheritance. It is the *improper use* of inheritance. It is using if statements or switches to handle special cases (such as "regular" and "foreign" students) or treating special cases in special ways. You end up with weakly cohesive code that is very difficult to change. This is exacerbated by certain "agile" approaches that tell developers not to look ahead, not to anticipate. That is bad advice. Do look ahead! Just be sure to look ahead at the right things. Don't look at the special cases, but rather look at the concepts they represent.

The problem with the nouns-and-verbs approach to modeling is that it does not address the real problem, which is identifying the entities in the problem domain in a way that keeps each of them separate from the other. If you cannot keep them separate, you end up with classes that have unrelated behaviors in them, resulting in weak cohesion and tight

---

4. When N things need to change and N>1, Shalloway will find at most N-1 of the things. See Chapter 4.

coupling. The bigger and more complex the code gets, the greater the coupling and the weaker the cohesion.

What is needed is an approach that helps keep separate those concepts that just happen to be discovered at the same time but have no other logical connection and to do this with a minimum of anticipation. Remember that in agile projects, even if we have the full problem in front of us, we want to spend only a short amount of time on the initial model.

What We Need to Know

What if we told you that we know a concept that would solve more than half of the problems you encounter when changing code? What if we told you that you, also, already know this concept but that you act like you don't? How would you feel? It's true! We know it and so do you. Here it is.

An example of something represents a concept of the thing, but the thing itself should not be taken for the concept.

Here is a simple example. At the start of many DVDs there is a message that says, "This movie has been formatted to fit your screen." Really? *My* screen? How did they even know the format of my screen? Oh, that's right, they meant screens *like* mine. *My* screen is one TV, but they were using "my screen" to represent the concept "TVs owned by the public." But you knew that.

Now, did you notice that we are not really talking about DVDs but rather about home video? They had this message on video tapes, too. So, our use of "DVD" actually stood for a broader concept: *video media* being played in the home.

Here is another example: On computers running Microsoft Windows (prior to Vista), that little "shut down" button at the lower left was used to shut down your computer. Click it, and you would find that it actually offers a number of choices, such as sleep, hibernate, and shut down. Perhaps it behaved this way because in the early of Windows, the only option to "change the power state of your computer" was to "shut down" the computer and so the option was labeled "Shut down." As new variations to "change the power state of your computer" were added, the label didn't change. It caused confusion in the user interface and maybe confusion in the code. How much confusion would have been avoided had they paid attention to the concept "change the power state" rather than the one example, "shut down."

We do this all the time in our speaking. We switch back and forth effortlessly between the example of a concept and the concept itself without noticing what we are doing. But in software, once something is modeled as an example or a concept, the code doesn't switch. We need a method that enables us to make this distinction clear. Otherwise, our code will become brittle and viscous.

Handling Variation

Let's step back for a minute. At the beginning of a project, you have only a cursory view of the problem. You know that you want to defer implementation details, but those details are mostly what you know. Is there a way to create an overall view that can do this without taking up too much time or requiring up-front design?

Begin by discovering the concepts that are present in the problem domain. Then find the implementations (or variations) of these concepts. And plan to handle variations of these concepts by encapsulating them.[5]

We need to be able to do this quickly and to be able to cope with minimal and incomplete information. The approach to use is called Commonality and Variability Analysis.

Commonality and Variability Analysis

Jim Coplien's work[6] describes an approach to finding variations in the problem domain and identifying what is common across the domain. Identify *where* things vary ("Commonality Analysis") and then identify *how* they vary ("Variability Analysis").

Commonality Analysis

According to Coplien, "Commonality Analysis is the search for common elements that helps us understand how family members are the same."[7] By "family members," Coplien means elements that are related to each other by the situation in which they appear or the function they

---

5. Encapsulating variation simply means hiding the implementation details behind an interface (either a literal interface type or a set of methods that establish its use). The code using this interface must treat everything that is behind the interface as if it were not varying; that is, the interface will describe the concept, and each of the implementations behind the interface will vary the implementation of that concept.
6. Coplien, James O. *Multi-Paradigm Design for C++*. Boston, MA: Addison-Wesley, 1998.
7. ibid, p. 63.

perform. The process of finding out how things are common defines the family in which these elements belong (and hence, where things vary).

For example, if I showed you a whiteboard marker, a pencil, and a ballpoint pen, you might say that what they all have in common is that they make marks on things, they have tips, they fit well in the hand, and so on. You may suggest the name "writing instruments" for anything that has these characteristics. The process you performed to identify them all in a common manner is Commonality Analysis.

Variability Analysis

These commonalities also make it easier to discuss how they are different. One difference is what these writing instruments can write on: a whiteboard or paper. Another difference is the materials that can be used for writing: erasable, permanent, graphite. Variability Analysis reveals how family members vary. Variability only makes sense within a given commonality.

> *Commonality analysis seeks structure that is unlikely to change over time, while variability analysis captures structure that is likely to change. Variability analysis makes sense only in terms of the context defined by the associated commonality analysis ... From an architectural perspective, commonality analysis gives the architecture its longevity; variability analysis drives its fitness for use.*[8]

In other words, variations are the specific concrete cases from the domain. Commonalities define the concepts in the domain that these variations are examples of. These common concepts will be represented by abstract type (abstract classes, interfaces, and so on). The variations found by Variability Analysis will be implemented by the concrete type, that is, entities implementing these abstract classes or interfaces.

Object-Oriented Design Captures All Three Perspectives

Consider Figure 10.3. It shows the relationship between the following:

- Commonality and Variability Analysis
- The conceptual, specification, and implementation perspectives
- An abstract class, its interface, and its derived classes

---

8. ibid, pp. 60, 64.

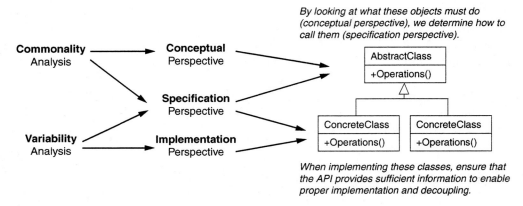

Figure 10.3   The relationship between Commonality and Variability Analysis, perspectives, and abstract classes

As you can see in Figure 10.3, Commonality Analysis relates to the conceptual view of the problem domain, and Variability Analysis relates to the implementation, that is, to specific cases.

Specification gives a better understanding of abstract classes.

The specification perspective lies in the middle. Both Commonality and Variability Analysis are involved in this perspective. The specification defines how to communicate with a set of objects that are conceptually similar. Each of these objects represents a variation of the common concept. This specification becomes an abstract type at the implementation level.

Note that the previous relationships hold true for Java/C# type interfaces as well. In fact, there are many ways to implement a concept. A commonality could be an attribute that varies by value, a regular expression that varies by specific string, and so on. Abstract base type and concrete derived types are only one way of modeling commonality Variability Analysis.

A New Paradigm for Finding Objects

Commonality-Variability Analysis offers a different way of decomposing the domain, resulting in decoupled concepts. Each of these concepts can be represented by an interface. The variations that are present can be implementations of this interface. The advantage of this approach is that we can provide more and more specializations while keeping classes decoupled and our class hierarchies relatively flat.

Note: For the remainder of this chapter, we will use the term "interface" to mean any of the methods of representing abstractions available in the different programming languages. This can be an abstract class or interface in Java or C# or a class with all pure virtual functions and no data members in C++. It could even be an interface that a template in C++ defines.[9] Decomposing the problem domain into concepts and implementations provides a three-step procedure for creating an overall, high-level map of your problem domain. The first is to identify the concepts, and the second is to see which variations of those concepts exist. Once these have been identified, the specification for the interfaces can be determined. This specification identifies the interface needed to handle all the cases of a concept (that is, the commonality defined by the conceptual perspective).

The relationship between the specification perspective and the implementation perspective is this: Given this specification, how can I implement this particular case (this variation)?

Tips for Finding Your Concepts and Variations with an Example

We have found two simple questions can be used to find concepts and variations. Pick anything in the problem domain. Now ask the following questions.

- Is this a concept or an implementation?

- If it is a concept, what are the variations of it? If it's an implementation, what is it a variation of?

For example, in the disk drive example discussed earlier, you might pick the C4DD_XYZ controller. Going through the two questions, you would get that the C4DD is an implementation of the concept "controller." And you would already have identified two classes: Controller

---

9. In *Multiparadigm Design for C++*, Jim Coplien discusses how template methods effectively define an interface since the class template has to implement the methods used in the template. One is effectively defining the behavior that a class has to support in order to be used by the template.

and C4DD. Now, pick something else. There are different encrypting algorithms. Ask the two questions, and you will realize that "encrypting algorithm" is a concept that has two implementations, Algorithm A and Algorithm B.

The Analysis Matrix: A Case Study

The notion of Commonality-Variability Analysis is easy to describe. To make it scale to the challenges we face in software development, you need one more tool. It is a simple and powerful tool called the "Analysis Matrix." The Analysis Matrix is a method of tracking requirements where one case can be specified at a time, each case adding more information to the understanding of the problem domain to be implemented. However, it is done in such a manner as to create greater clarity on the concepts in the problem domain while keeping track of each specific implementation method used for each case.

The matrix is built as follows:

1. Select a specific example to be described.

2. List the steps required to be implemented for this case with the first step at the top and with each subsequent step underneath the prior step.

3. Create a column to the left of the step being described.

4. As you list each step, put the concept that the step relates to its left.

Table 10.1 illustrates this first sequence of steps for a sales-order system in the United States.

Table 10.1   Steps in a Sales-Order System

Concept	Case 1: Sales Processing in the United States
Create a record.	Create a new sales order record.
Find customer.	Enter the customer for which this sales order is for.
Update customer.	Provide an option to update information on the selected customer.

Table 10.1   Steps in a Sales-Order System (*Continued*)

Concept	Case 1: Sales Processing in the United States
Select items.	Select items to be purchased.
Select shipment.	Select how to ship.
Calculate tax.	Use local tax codes to calculate tax.
Select payment.	Select payment type.
Process.	Process sales order.

Each case (column) can be a story that implements some functionality. In this example, the first case is for processing a sales order in the United States.

Now, find another case, add a column to the right, and do the same thing. Each entry should specify how the concept in the leftmost column is implemented. For an example, see Table 10.2.

Table 10.2   Adding Steps to Process a Sales Order in Canada

Concept	Case 1: Sales Processing in the United States	Case 2: Sales Processing in Canada
Create a record.	Create a new sales order record.	"
Find customer.	Enter the customer that this sales order is for.	"
Update customer.	Provide an option to update information on the selected customer.	"
Select items.	Select items to be purchased.	"
Select shipment.	Select how to ship.	"

continues

Table 10.2 Adding Steps to Process a Sales Order in Canada (*Continued*)

Concept	Case 1: Sales Processing in the United States	Case 2: Sales Processing in Canada
Calculate tax.	Use local tax codes to calculate tax.	Use GST and PST.
Select payment.	Select payment type.	"
Process.	Process sales order.	"

Notice how entries that are the same as the entry in the left column (for example, creating a new sales-order record) can be marked with a " to make it clear that that is the case. However, one should ask whether this is really the case. The "Update customer" row will actually be different because customer information for the United States is different from customer information in Canada (the address being one example). You may also have different shipping methods in Canada. In that case, you would modify Table 10.2 to be what is shown in Table 10.3 (italics highlighting the changes).

Note that two things are happening here. First, as you gain clarity on one case, it reflects on the other cases. Second, you will start seeing the

Table 10.3 Adding Steps to Show New Shipping Methods

Concept	Case 1: Sales Processing in the United States	Case 2: Sales Processing in Canada
Create a record.	Create a new sales order record.	"
Find customer.	Enter the customer that this sales order is for.	"
Update customer.	Provide an option to update information on the selected U.S. customer.	*Provide an option to update information on the selected Canadian customer.*

continues

Table 10.3   Adding Steps to Show New Shipping Methods (*Continued*)

Concept	Case 1: Sales Processing in the United States	Case 2: Sales Processing in Canada
Select items.	Select items to be purchased.	"
Select shipment.	Select how to ship *using list of U.S. freight carriers.*	Select how to ship *using list of Canadian freight carriers.*
Calculate tax.	Use local tax codes to calculate tax.	Use GST and PST.
Select payment.	Select payment type.	"
Process.	Process sales order.	"

differences in implementation between the cases. As you discover new concepts, add them as new rows in the table.

Table 10.4 shows what happens when you add another case, a sales order in Germany.

Notice the two additional rows: one for date formats and one for a maximum shipping weight.

- The date format is something we should have noticed before but didn't. This is one of the powers of the matrix: As you add more columns to the right, you will get more rows as each specific case uncovers more concepts.

- "Specify maximum shipping weight" shows something we discovered that was missing. Discovering missing concepts by merely talking to customers (or their proxies) is often difficult because it is hard to know what you've left out. In any event, once one has been discovered, it is easy enough to ask: "What are the maximum weights allowed for shipping in the United States and in Canada?"

Using the matrix, you will find that as you add more cases, you will find more concepts. So, when do you stop? Do you really need all of the cases? Actually, you don't. What you want to find is the concepts that are present. So, once you stop adding rows (concepts) as you add more

Table 10.4 Adding Another Case

Concept	Case: Sales Processing in the United States	Case 2: Sales Processing in Canada	Case 3: Sales Processing in Germany
Create a record.	Create a new sales order record.	"	"
Find customer.	Enter the customer that this sales order is for.	"	"
Update customer.	Provide an option to update information on the selected U.S. customer.	Provide an option to update information on the selected Canadian customer.	Provide an option to update information on the selected German customer.
Select items.	Select items to be purchased.	"	"
Select shipment.	Select how to ship using list of U.S. freight carriers.	Select how to ship using list of Canadian freight carriers.	Select how to ship using list of German freight carriers.
Calculate tax.	Use local tax codes to calculate tax.	Use GST and PST.	VAT.
Select payment.	Select payment type.	"	"
Specify date formats.	mm/dd/yyyy.	dd/mm/yyyy.	dd/mm/yyyy.
Specify maximum shipping weight.	??	??	30 kg.
Process.	Process sales order.	"	"

cases (columns), you can feel reasonably assured that you have found most of the concepts.

Selecting the Stories to Analyze

When it comes to picking stories to analyze, do it intentionally, not randomly. Select stories that will give a good representation of the concepts involved. For example, here is an example of the analysis matrix I (Alan) created while consulting at Boeing.[10] McDonnell Douglas, a domestic airline, had requested that Boeing create a method of pulling up all of the information needed to do maintenance on a particular plane when the airline's system indicated maintenance was needed. To do this, the system would need to be able to integrate the following document-retrieval systems.

- **Plane Manufacturers**
  - Boeing
  - McDonnell Douglas
- **Engine Manufacturers**
  - GE
  - Rolls Royce
  - Pratt & Whitney
- **Domestic Airlines**
  - Continental
  - American Airlines
  - Southwest Airlines
  - Alaska Airlines
  - Delta
- **European Airlines**
  - British Airways
  - Easy Jet

---

10. Note: We can talk about this because this problem was in the public since it involved many different airlines. That is, no NDA is being breached here.

- **Asian Carriers**
  - China Airlines
  - Japan Airlines
  - Korean Airlines
- **Other Carriers**
  - Egypt Air
  - El Al
  - Emirates
- **Aircraft Component Makers**
  - Galley Mfr 1
  - Galley Mfr 2
  - Galley Mfr 3
  - Toilet Mfr 1
  - Toilet Mfr 2
  - Water closet Mfr 1
  - Water closet Mfr 2
  - Water closet Mfr 3
  - Vendor X
  - Vendor Y

As you can see, there are many different cases to consider! Which ones would you select? Would we need to consider them all? Or just a selected set? If we decided just to do a selected set, how would we select them? We could just go down the list—that is, do Boeing, McDonnell Douglas, GE, Rolls Royce, and so on—until we stop adding new rows. Or, we could just pick them randomly until we stop adding new rows. Or, we can think about it a little first.[11]

---

11. At this point, the authors are reminded of a favorite Deming quote—"Don't just do something, stand there"—whereupon he meant it is often worth considering one's course of action before undertaking it.

Notice that a document-control system for a domestic carrier is more likely to be similar to another domestic carrier than it is, say, to an engine manufacturer or even a foreign carrier. Hence, when selecting cases, I decided to select them based on the type of company for which the document-control system was written. These are shown in italics in the following list.

- **Plane Manufacturers**
  - *Boeing*
  - *McDonnell Douglas*[12]
- **Engine Manufacturers**
  - *GE*
  - Rolls Royce
  - Pratt & Whitney
- **Domestic Airlines**
  - *Continental*
  - American Airlines
  - Southwest Airlines
  - Alaska Airlines
  - Delta
- **European Airlines**
  - *British Airways*
  - Easy Jet
- **Asian Carriers**
  - *China Airlines*
  - Japan Airlines
  - Korean Airlines

---

12. Note the exception here in that we're doing both Boeing and McDonnell Douglas since we'll be needing to handle these two systems and these are most likely the biggest ones present.

- **Other Carriers**
  - *Egypt Air*
  - El Al
  - Emirates
- **Aircraft Component Makers**
  - *Galley Mfr 1*
  - Galley Mfr 2
  - Galley Mfr 3
  - *Toilet Mfr 1*
  - Toilet Mfr 2
  - *Water closet Mfr 1*
  - Water closet Mfr 2
  - Water closet Mfr 3
  - *Vendor X*
  - Vendor Y

Work through the list for each category (for example, engine manufacturers, domestic airlines) and pick one. When a selected case doesn't add a new concept, skip that category in the next pass. Although this is not an exact method, it should help us identify most of the concepts relatively quickly.

The Analysis Matrix has several uses. First, it helps us gain greater clarity about the problem domain while illustrating gaps and inconsistencies. Second, it helps developers realize that although the customer may be talking specifics, there will be other cases, and they need to prepare for them.[13] Finally, it illustrates the differences between the cases.

---

13. Doing this does not require a lot of extra code. The methods we've been discussing throughout this book (encapsulation, encapsulating construction, Programming by Intention) are more than sufficient to enable us to implement the specific cases while keeping the code easily modifiable for additional cases. This provides us with a way to write emergent code. That is, we can implement one case only paying attention to it but encapsulating the actual implementation in preparation for the next. This typically does not take any extra time; it merely requires avoiding coupling the calling routines from the implementations through a well-defined interface.

This can help determine the order in which to implement each of the cases (or stories).

The Analysis Matrix is quick to do, on the order of one to two days for a three- or six-month project with a team of ten people. The time required is more than paid back by the clarity it provides the team as well as the general application architecture it provides. In other words, the Analysis Matrix enables a quick conceptual design of the problem domain model.

Summary

Many developers tend to use a "noun-and-verb" approach to modeling objects in the problem domain because it is how they were taught and it is pretty easy to do. Unfortunately, the method does not work very well for long. Soon it couples together essentially unrelated concepts, making adding any new ones very difficult.

Commonality-Variability Analysis helps developers avoid coupling between objectives by making it clear that our implementations are special cases and that new special cases will arrive shortly. By treating our objects as special cases of a more general concept that may not be clear yet, we decouple these known implementations from the objects that use them. The best approach is to encapsulate implementations and let the architecture handle more and more special cases as they emerge over time.

The Analysis Matrix is a quick, easy tool that supports Commonality-Variability Analysis. It enables a quick conceptual design of the problem domain model.

CHAPTER 11

Refactor to the Open-Closed

Solving tricky problems can often involve changing your point of view. In this chapter, we'll examine one particularly tricky problem: how to avoid overdesign without suffering the problems that often accompany an insufficient or naïve design. In the process, we'll rethink two, hopefully well-known, aspects of development: the Open-Closed principle and the discipline of refactoring. We'll begin by examining these aspects as they are traditionally understood and then repurpose them in a more agile way.

The Open-Closed Principle

The notion that systems have to accommodate change is not a new one. At the birth of objects and OO, Ivar Jacobsen said, "All systems change during their life cycles. This must be borne in mind when developing systems expected to last longer than the first version."[1] Of course, since this was before the invention of object-oriented languages and systems, he was focused on the particular nature of procedural code and how one can make code more or less "changeable" depending on what one focused upon when writing it.

Jacobsen was one of many who promoted the idea of breaking up programming functionality into multiple, "helper" functions, called from a central location in the code, with the idea that change would be fundamentally easier to deal with if code was not written in large "blobs." Without this, code would be hard to understand, hard to control in terms of side effects, and difficult to debug—hard to change, in other words.

---

1. Jacobson, Ivar, et al. *Object-Oriented Software Engineering: A Use Case Driven Approach.* Reading, MA: Addison-Wesley, 1993.

We still believe in this notion, and in fact it has become known today as the practice of Programming by Intention (see Chapter 1, Programming by Intention, for more details). Personally, we never write code any other way.

With the advent of OO, the same notion, namely, that we should expect our systems to change, took on a potentially different meaning. Bertrand Meyer, an early OO thinker and the creator of one of the most object-oriented languages of the time, Eiffel, rephrased Jacobsen this way:

> *Software entities (classes, modules, functions, etc.) should be open for extension, but closed for modification.*

Initially this was seen as a natural outgrowth of inheritance. If we have an existing class, let's call it ClassA, and we want to change some aspect of its behavior, it was pointed out that rather than making code changes to ClassA, we could instead create a new class based on it, through inheritance, and make the change(s) in the new class (see Figure 11.1).

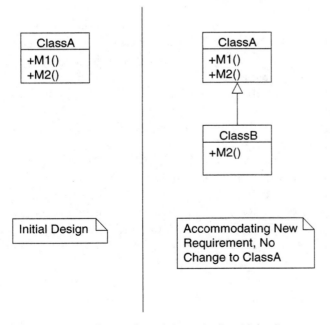

Figure 11.1   Open-closed through direct inheritance

ClassA, here, is an existing class with existing behavior. Now, we need something similar but with a variation in method M2(), so we've used inheritance to make a new class (ClassB) based on the existing one.

This was thought to be "reusing" the object and seemed to be an admirable aspect of OO. Leave ClassA alone, and you're not very likely to break it. A new class, ClassB, will contain only what is different and new (in this case, by overriding the M2() method) and will therefore also be simpler and safer to work with. This is most likely what caused the creators of Java to use the word "extends" to indicate inheritance, because Java was created in the early- to mid-1990s when just this sort of thinking was prevalent.

There were problems with this once developers started to see "inheritance for reuse" as the solution to essentially everything (see Chapter 13, When and How to Use Inheritance, for more details on this). Patterns, and the general design advice they contain, tended to make us reconsider what it meant to be "closed for modification" and to use class polymorphism to achieve it, as shown in Figure 11.2.

Now we can accommodate a new version of the M2_Service by adding another class, M2_Service_V2, and make no changes to the existing code in ClassA or in M2_Service_V1. This means we are "open to extension" (adding a new class, in this case) and "closed to modification" (all the things we are not changing).

But even in the initial design, we have added a class (the abstract class M2_Service), and this is without considering how the initial M2_Service_V1 class will be instantiated.

If ClassA contains the code new M2_Service_V1() within it, then we would not be able to add M2_Service_V2 without changing that bit of code, and thus we would not be "closed to modification" of ClassA, which was our goal. In other words, the M2_Service abstract type does not really buy us much if client classes build concrete instances themselves. See Chapter 2, Separate Use from Construction, for a more detailed treatment of this topic.

To fix that problem, we'd have to add yet another entity, one that was solely responsible for creating the instance in the first place, and we would thereby know that was the one and only place where a code change would have to be made (see Figure 11.3). ClassA and all other clients of this service (reuse being another primary goal here) would not change when the V2 version came along.

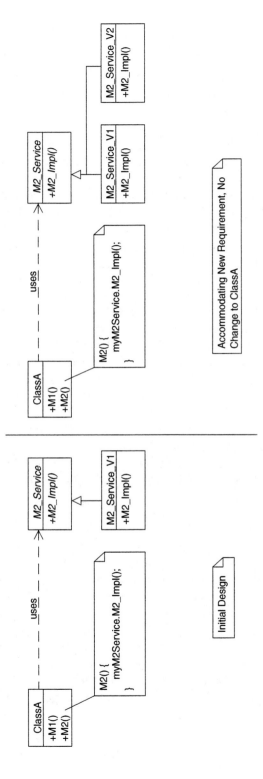

Figure 11.2 Open-closed through class polymorphism

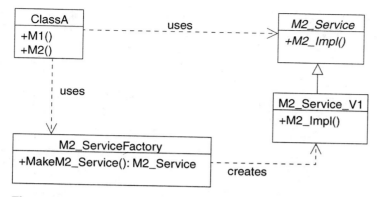

Figure 11.3   Adding an instantiation entity ("factory") to build the right instance

This would seem to be adding complexity for something that may or may not happen. In the past, we would often say to add this sort of antici-patory infrastructure when the issue was "likely to change," but there are few developers indeed who would claim to be able to make that estima-tion with any degree of confidence. Anticipatory guessing is not very reli-able and not repeatable over time. We need something more than luck.

Open-Closed to Other Things

Furthermore, people often focus on the Open-Closed principle in terms of adding a new behavior to an existing system. The truth is that the principle can apply to any change at all.

- An object may start out using a single instance of a service object and then later require more than one for load balancing or where there are different versions of a service and more than one version is needed. One→one versus one→many is a potential change.

- An object may use a set of service objects in a given order today and then alter the order tomorrow. The sequence of a workflow is a potential change.

- An object may be responsible for cleaning up the memory of the service object it holds, and then later it may no longer be. Memory management is a potential change.

- An object may use the same service object it was initially given throughout its life cycle and then later must have the ability to change the service object later. Static versus dynamic relationships is a potential change.

These are just a few examples. We should consider the Open-Closed principle as potentially applying to all of these circumstances. When any of these potential changes occurs, we'd like to be able to accommodate it by adding something new and leaving as much of the existing system as is.

But as before, the question is how can we know when any of these changes are likely enough that it is worth putting in the extra abstractions, factories, and so forth up front?

Open-Closed Is a "Principle"

Principles can be thought of either being rules of nature (or programming in our case) or guidance to follow to best take advantage of these rules. Principles are always true, but how to use them depends upon the context in which you find yourself. The principle does not specify a specific tactic for achieving this, because there are many that could work, depending on circumstance.

Remember that the Open-Closed principle comes from Jacobsen's notion that all systems will have to be changed and that this was before the creation of objects and object-oriented languages and tools. So, what he was referring to was the basic way code is structured, using the finer-grained functions mentioned earlier.

For a concrete example of what Jacobsen was recommending, we can turn to something fun.

Several years ago, when IBM was trying to encourage some of their older, quite experienced developers to switch to an object-oriented point of view (in this case, by learning Java), they ran into some resistance. These guys felt that they could do what they needed to do without OO and really didn't want to have to abandon their tried-and-true techniques in procedural code. This is understandable; good procedural code required a lot of discipline and experience, and so these guys had invested a lot of themselves into it.

So, IBM tapped into the generally competitive nature of most software developers. They came up with a game, called "Robocode,"[2] which allowed developers to write Java classes that would actually fight each

---

2. Robocode is more complex than we are intimating here, but this makes our point. For more, visit their site! It's wicked fun: http://robocode.sourceforge.net/.

other, with explosions and all, in a graphical framework. The devs write the classes; the game lets them fight each other.

The following is an example of a *very* simple Robocode robot class.

```
import robocode.*;
public class Robbie extends Robot {
  public void run() {
    ahead(100);
    turnGunRight(360);
    back(100);
    turnGunRight(360);
  }

  public void onScannedRobot(RobotEvent re) {
    if(isNotMyTeam(re)) fire(1);
  }
}
```

By extending Robot, Robbie can be upcast to that type, and the game will be able to call methods like `run()` when it's Robbie's turn to move and `onScannedRobot()` when Robbie sees an enemy, and so on.

You might have noticed that neither of these methods really does much in and of itself. `run()` called other methods like `ahead()`, `turnGun-Right()`, and so forth. `onScannedRobot()` delegates to other methods as well. Jacobsen and others of the time called these subordinate methods "helper methods," and they suggested that this was a good practice to follow.

It's good because adding more helper methods, removing existing ones, or changing the implementation of a helper method, and so on, can have very limited impact on the rest of the system. Contrast this to how such changes would play out if `run()` had all the code in it, in a large, complicated structure. Such structures will work, but they are very hard to change later.

Would this design be more open-closed if these behaviors, like `fire()`, were in separate objects? Sure. But how far do you go?

One extreme would be to pull everything out into its own object. This would create vast numbers of small objects, creating a lot of complexity and coupling. The other extreme is to code all behavior into a single method in a single object. Neither seems very attractive, so how do we find the best middle ground? One adds flexibility at the expense of complexity; the other loses code quality. How can we add flexibility when we need it? That's what refactoring to the open-closed will allow us to do.

Refactoring

It's not uncommon for developers to make changes to code that make no difference or cause no changes in the behavior of a system. Sometimes, for instance, we may change the name of a variable, clean up the indentation in nest logic, give a method a more intention-revealing name, or change a code structure to make it easier to read (a for loop replaced with `foreach` loop), and so on.

Sometimes these changes can actually alter a design or architecture, but again, they may not change the outward-facing functionality of the system from the stakeholder's point of view or in the way it interacts with or affects other systems.

When we make such a change, we are refactoring. We make this distinct from *enhancing* a system, *debugging* it, or taking any other action that would change its resulting behavior (including, of course *breaking* it).

In his ground-breaking book *Refactoring*,[3] Martin Fowler defined a specific set of disciplines around what had up to that point been individual, ad hoc practices. He defined his "refactoring moves" in a way quite similar to design patterns; take things we do repeatedly, give them specific names, and capture what we as a community know about them so this knowledge becomes shared. We often think of refactoring moves as "patterns of change." They establish a shared language that communicates our plans and expectations with a higher degree of fidelity.

Extract Method, for example, would be the refactoring move that we'd use to convert a "single method blob" of code into the "helper method" approach used in our Robot earlier. If we realized that one of those helper methods actually should be in its own class, we could do Extract Class if the class was a new one or Move Method if we were moving it to an existing class. In each case, a clearly defined series of steps is defined, making sure that we don't miss anything critical and enabling us to improve the code aggressively and with high confidence. It's an enormously useful book.

That said, refactoring has gotten something of a bad reputation among those who pay for software to be developed.

If a development team is "refactoring the system" business owners know that they can expect no new functionality or improved performance from the system while this is going on. In fact, every refactoring move includes running a suite of tests to *ensure* that nothing has

---

3. Fowler, Martin. *Refactoring: Improving the Design of Existing Code.* Reading, MA: Addison-Wesley, 1999.

changed in the way the system behaves. The same tests must pass after the refactoring that passed before it.

This reputation is understandable. Refactoring improves the design of a system, in terms of its source code. Only the developers encounter the source code, so obviously refactoring is a developer-centric activity and delivers value only to developers...or so it would seem.

Also, there is no end to refactoring, per se. No system design is ever perfect, and therefore any system could be refactored to improve its design. Making these improvements can be a very rewarding, satisfying, and intellectually stimulating thing for a developer to do, so it is possible to fall into the trap of obsessively refactoring a system.

Why Refactor?

As part of the discipline, Fowler included a set of "code smells" to help us to see where refactoring improvements are called for.

If we find that we're making the same change in many different places, he calls this "shotgun surgery." If we find that a method in Class A is referring to the state or functionality of Class B to an excessive degree, he calls this "feature envy." A class that has no functionality but does contain state is called "lazy," and so on. These smells do not necessarily indicate a problem but rather a potential problem that should be investigated and refactored if appropriate.

These smells, in other words, help us target parts of the system that could be refactored and, arguably, improved, but what they do not tell is if the system *should be refactored now.* When is it worth it, and when are we, in fact, falling into the trap that has given refactoring a bad reputation among those who pay for software to be developed?

Debt versus Investment

Let's make a distinction about this decision. Do we fix something in the design of the code, even though the code is working?

If we see something we know is "not good code" and we decide not to fix it, we know two things:

- If we do not fix it, we save time and can move on to adding new functionality to the system. However, this new functionality will be achieved at the cost of leaving the poor code in place.

- If we fix the code at a later point in time, it will likely cost more. It will probably have gotten worse, more things will be coupled to it the way it is now, and it will be less fresh in our minds (requiring more time to reinvestigate the issue).

Doing something that avoids payment now at the cost of a higher payment later is essentially "debt." It's like buying something on your credit card. It is not that you don't *ever* have to pay for it; you just don't have to pay for it now. Later, when you do, there will be interest added, and it will cost you more.

If, on the other hand, we fix the bad code without adding any outward business value to the system, we must acknowledge that this is not "free"; it costs money (our customer's money). However, we also know the following:

- Cleaner code is easier to change. Therefore, changes we are asked to make later will be easier to do, take less time, and therefore save money.

- This can pay off over and over again, as one change leads to another or as the business continually requires new functionality from the system.

In other words, this constitutes an investment. Pay now, and then get paid back over and over again in the future. It's a little like the notion of the "money tree." When you plant the tree, initially you don't get anything for your effort. Once the tree grows into blossom, however, it pays off over and over again.

Businesses understand these concepts very well. They will accept debt consciously, but they know that holding a valuable investment is preferable. Sometimes it helps to speak the language of the person you're trying to influence.

Refactoring and Legacy Systems

Most people think of refactoring in terms of "cleaning up" legacy code. Such code was often written with a focus on making the system as small and fast as possible. Computers in the earlier days often made this a necessity; sure, the code is incomprehensible and impossible to maintain when we come back to it later, but it was easier for the slower computers to deal with, and computers were the critical resource in those days, not developers.

Legacy systems that have remained in place, however, have probably proved their value by the very fact that they are still here. Fowler's initial purpose was to take this code that has value in one sense (what it *does*) and to reshape it into code that is valuable in the more modern sense (we can work with it efficiently), without removing any of that exiting value, that is, without harming it.

Refactoring to the Open-Closed

So, refactoring is often thought of in terms of bad code, untested code, and code that has decayed over time and that we have to suffer with now.

This is true as far as it goes. However, we also know that it's very difficult to predict what changes will come along, and that change can appear almost anywhere in our process.

- Requirements can change.

- Technology can change.

- The marketplace can change.

- Our organization/team can change.

- We change (ideally, we get smarter).

These are just a few examples. So, another role for refactoring skills to play is when we have code that *was fine yesterday* but it is not easy to modify in the light of a particular changing circumstance. In other words, we have something new that we need to add now to the code, but we cannot add it in an open-closed fashion as it stands.

Let's use our Robocode Robot as a concrete example. The design so far is a simple, single class that extends a type called Robot (see Figure 11.4).

This is not open-closed in terms of adding new classes to change behaviors. If we come up with more than one way of "firing," for instance (maybe we'll have more than one kind of gun in the future), we'll have to change the code in the fire() method, perhaps adding a switch or other logic to accommodate the variation in behavior. Similarly, if we get new ways of turning, moving, or determining whether another Robot is on "my team," we'll have to make code changes, and we'll add complexity when we do.

To make it open-closed in the senses that we usually mean today, we'd introduce polymorphism for all of these behaviors. The design would probably look something like what is presented in Figure 11.5.

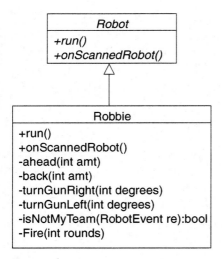

Figure 11.4   Robbie the Robot

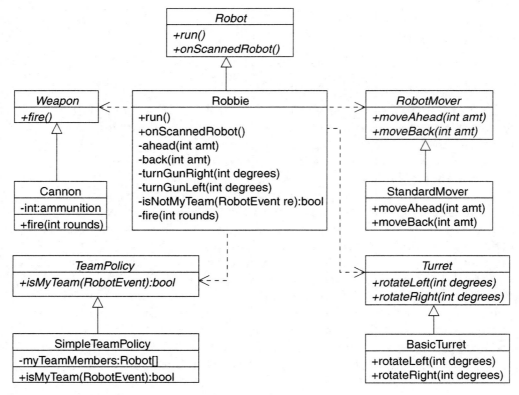

Figure 11.5   Everything is open-closed.

This would make it possible for us to add a different kind of weapon, turret, movement mechanism, or team structure without having to alter the code in Robot. But, given that none of these things is varying right now, this is far more complex than we need, especially when you consider that we have not added those factories yet!

If you feel, given that none of these behaviors are varying at the moment, that this approach is overdoing it, we'd agree. If we pull out all possible variations, as a rote practice, we will tend to produce designs that are overly complex.

Some would say that we should pull out issues that are not varying today but are *likely to vary* in the future. The problem with this predictive approach is that we're likely to be wrong too often, and when we are, we will have pulled something out that never varies (overdesign) and fail to pull the thing out that needs to be variable (failing to be open-closed).

In studying refactoring, we are learning how to make changes in a disciplined way. Each refactoring, though it may have been originally intended as a way to clean up bad code, can also be used to change code *just enough* to allow it to be changed in an open-closed way, once we know this change is necessary.

We call this "refactoring to the open-closed."

Just-in-Time Design

Refactoring to the open-closed allows us to introduce design elements as they are needed but not before. It allows design to emerge in a just-in-time way, which means we can proceed based on what we know and when we know it, rather than through prediction.

Look back at the version of Robbie in Figure 11.4. Let's say we designed and coded it that way and then later a new requirement emerged: We need to be able to accommodate a new kind of "fire" mechanism (a new weapon or a new way of firing in general). We could put a switch into the fire() method of Robbie, but this is not an open-closed change.

In the light of this new requirement (which is not a guess but is actually being requested), we can do this in stages, using our refactoring skills. First, we do Extract Class,[4] as shown in Figure 11.6.

---

4. Fowler, Martin. *Refactoring: Improving the Design of Existing Code.* Reading, MA: Addison-Wesley, 1999.

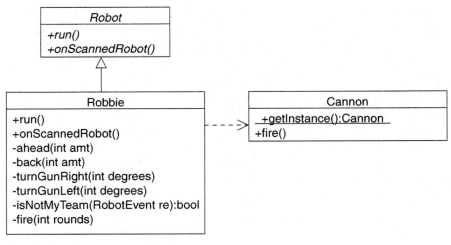

Figure 11.6   Extract Class

(You'll note that we've used a static `getInstance()` method to create the instance of `Cannon`. See Chapter 2, Separate Use from Construction, for more on this technique.)

The `fire()` method in Robbie now contains a call to the `fire()` method in Cannon. This is still not open-closed, but we're getting closer. Next, we do Extract Interface, as shown in Figure 11.7.[5]

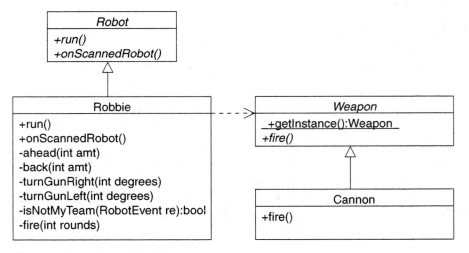

Figure 11.7   Extract Interface

---

5. Fowler, Martin. *Refactoring: Improving the Design of Existing Code.* Reading, MA: Addison-Wesley, 1999.

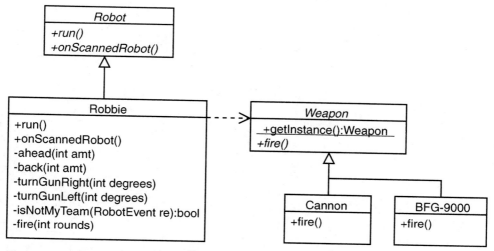

Figure 11.8   Extract Interface

We have not changed the behavior of the Robot, and if we had tests running, they would still all pass in the same way. This is one nice thing about automated tests; they confirm that we are, in fact, refactoring, not enhancing or introducing bugs.

This is now open-closed to the new weapon, and we are done refactoring. Now we can enhance the system with the new requirement in an open-closed way, as shown in Figure 11.8.

Summary

Basing your decisions on prediction is setting yourself up to fail. Trying to design for every possible future change will lead to overdesign, which is also setting yourself up to fail.

The refactoring discipline, used to enable this just-in-time response to changes, allows you to make your decision based on what actually happens, not what you predict will happen, and also allows you to introduce design elements as you need them, avoiding overdesign.

So, what's missing? Tests. Refactoring requires automated testing, because it is the tests that tell you whether you are, in fact, refactoring. See Chapter 3, Define Tests Up Front, for more on testing.

CHAPTER 12

Needs versus Capabilities Interfaces

One challenge facing development is the creation of strongly encapsulating interfaces. Even if the argument "design to interfaces" is accepted as common wisdom by a team, still the exact nature and placement of those interfaces can be hard to get "right." In this chapter, we will examine the notion of the interface and show how our desire to control dependencies can give us the right point of view from which to discover strong interfaces.

The Law of Demeter

Controlling dependencies is not a new problem. System maintenance has always been critical, and dependencies can make changes very difficult when a change to one part of a system may ripple through other parts through the coupling that exists between them. In 1982[1] Karl Lieberherr began experimenting with language constructs that might assist us in limiting dependencies, and this led eventually to a project at Northwestern University called Project Demeter, which focuses on adaptive languages.

While working on the project, Lieberherr and Ian Holland noticed a problem in object models that can be illustrated fairly simply. Consider the model of a typical city grid shown in Figure 12.1.

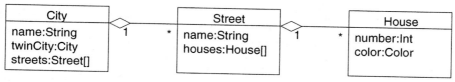

Figure 12.1   Model of a city grid

---

1. http://en.wikipedia.org/wiki/Law_of_Demeter

```
public class City {
  public string name{};
  public City twinCity{};
  public Street[] streets{};
}
public class Street {
  public string name{};
  public House[] houses{};
}
public class House {
  public int number{};
  public Color color{};
}
```

Simply put, a `City` has a name and a twin city reference and consists of a collection of `Streets`. A `Street` has a name and consists of a collection of Houses. A House has a number and a color.

Models like this encourage us to expose rather than to encapsulate. If your code has a reference to a particular `City` instance, say one that maps Seattle, and you wanted the color of the house at 1374 Main Street, then you might do something like the following:

```
public Foo() {
  Color c = Seattle.streets()["Main"].
    houses()[1374].
    color();
}
```

The problem, if this is done as a general practice, is that the system develops dependencies everywhere, and a change to any part of this model can have effects up and down the chain of these dependencies.

That's where the Law of Demeter, which states[2] "Don't talk to strangers," comes in. This is formalized in object systems as the Law of Demeter for Functions/Methods.

> A method M of an object O may only invoke the methods of the following kinds of objects:
>
> 1. O's
> 2. M's parameters
> 3. Any objects instantiated within M
> 4. O's direct component objects
> 5. Any global variables accessible by O

---

2. http://en.wikipedia.org/wiki/Law_of_Demeter

So, for example, the following code complies with the Law of Demeter for functions/methods.

```
public City theCapital;

public class CityUser {
  public City aCityFooKnows;

  public string Foo(City aCityFooIsGiven){
    City aCityFooInstantiated = instantiateCity();

    return + cityName() +               // case 1
      aCityFooIsGiven.name() +          // case 2
      aCityFooInstantiated.name() +     // case 3
      aCityFooKnows.name() +            // case 4
      theCapital.name;                  // Case 5
  }
  public string cityName() {/*…*/}
}
```

Foo() follows the law in that it interacts only with state on its class (aCityFooKnows), state that was passed to it by the caller (aCityFooIsGiven), or state that it created (aCityFooCreates).

Our previous Foo implementation interacted with state (color) that belonged to another entity (house), which itself was not our state but state on another entity (street) that was state on Foo's class. It is a cascading dependency.

The Law of Demeter would suggest something like the following:

```
public Foo() {
  Color c = Seattle.ColorOfHouseInStreet("Main",1374);
}
```

The City's interface is now hiding the implementation that allows for access to the color of a given house. Foo is interacting only with a state member of its own class. Sometimes people summarize this as "play only with your own toys."

Although this would seem to be a wise policy initially, it can quickly get out of hand as the interface of any given entity can be expected to provide literally anything it relates to. These interfaces tend to bloat over time, and in fact there would seem to be almost no end to the number of public methods a given glass may eventually support.

The Law of Demeter actually *is* a sound principle, but we need to dig into the issues that motivate it a bit more. It really has to do with the nature of coupling and dependencies.

Coupling, Damned Coupling, and Dependencies

Coupling is required for systems to operate. In one sense, a system *is* coupling. In object systems, this is reflected in the relationship where one object messages another. We usually think of them as the `Client` and `Service` objects in this relationship, as shown in Figure 12.2.

The vulnerability here is that any change to the `Service`'s public access points can cause a needed change in the `Client`. We often call this "tight" coupling because of this fact.

Coupling and Testability

Another hint that this can be problematic arises when we attempt to test `Client`. A test for `Client` requires the presence of `Service`, so knowledge on how to create, initialize, and bring `Service` to the needed state for the test to commence is required. Moreover, said test can fail when `Client` is working just fine but `Service` has a bug. Just as bad, assuming `Service` has its own test, then when `Service` has a bug, you will see at least *two* tests failing: the test of `Service` and the test of `Client`. We prefer tests that fail singly, leading us immediately to the location of the defect.

This leads us to create a separate interface for the relationship (see Figure 12.3).

Both `Client` and `ServiceImpl` are vulnerable to a change in `Service` (`Client` because it would have to use `Service` differently, `ServiceImpl` because it would have to implement `Service` differently), but since `Service` is *only* an interface (and would not be tested in and of itself), then we can create the isolation we're seeking.

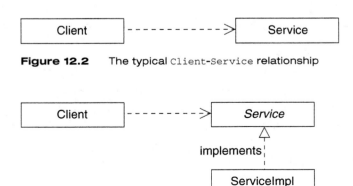

Figure 12.2   The typical `Client-Service` relationship

Figure 12.3   `Client` coupled to the interface of `Service` only

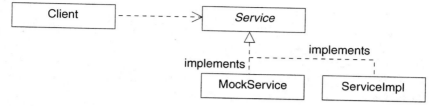

Figure 12.4   Loose coupling creates opportunities to isolate entities for testing.

A test of `ServiceImpl` does not require `Client`. A test of `Client` can be conducted without the actual `ServiceImpl` as well, by using a simple mock object (see Figure 12.4).

Here again, `Client`, `ServiceImpl`, and `MockService` are only vulnerable to changes in the interface `Service`, which has no implementation in it. There is another vulnerability, however, that is often not immediately clear but that will become clear later when a second `Client` for the same service is created.

Needs versus Capabilities

We expect this. In fact, one could say that the day a second `Client` appears for the same `Service`, we have just doubled the value of the `Service` and the effort it took to create it (see Figure 12.5). The more `Client`s, the more value is harvested from that effort.

The vulnerability we may have missed is this: If this new $Client_2$ requires something different in `Service`, perhaps access to a new return, the ability to pass it a new parameter, or an entirely new service method, then this need can cause/require a change in $Client_1$.

We seem to have simply pushed our vulnerability around and hidden it in a more subtle place. However, if we add one more idea to our model here, we can solve this, too.

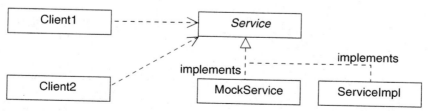

Figure 12.5   A second client validates the value of the service but illustrates our hidden vulnerability.

Service is a *capabilities interface*. It reflects what Service can *do*. However, in this model it is also a *needs interface*, in that it reflects what Client$_1$ needs. Client$_2$ may have a different need or view of the same need, and therein lies the rub.

By creating separate interfaces for needs and capabilities, we can essentially eliminate all coupling to implementations.

The Ideal Separation: Needs Interfaces and Capabilities Interfaces

If we return to the single client model, we can instead create a more complete separation using the Adapter pattern, as shown in Figure 12.6.

Service reflects everything ServiceImpl can do. Needs$_1$ reflects what Client$_1$ wants, with an adapter (ServiceAdapter$_1$) making the translation. Note that Needs$_1$ can be mocked to test Client$_1$, and Service$_1$ can be mocked to test ServiceAdapter$_1$. No entity requires a concrete implementation of another entity when testing it, which simply reflects that there is no concrete coupling in this design.

The vulnerabilities are, therefore, the following:

- Needs$_1$ will change if Client$_1$'s needs changes. This makes sense: It reflects his needs.

- ServiceAdapter$_1$ will change if Needs$_1$ changes, or Service changes, but neither of these are implementations.

- ServiceImpl will change if Service changes, but this is unlikely since Clients do not couple to it.

- Client$_1$ is vulnerable to nothing, including a second Client's appearance in the future, as shown in Figure 12.7.

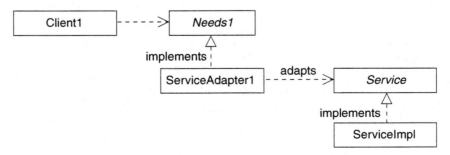

Figure 12.6   An adapter is used to separate needs from capabilities.

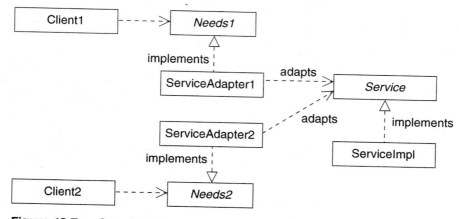

Figure 12.7   Complete separation of needs from capabilities

You may be thinking that this seems like a lot of complexity to create just in case Client₂ *might* arrive later, and you'd be right. But if you add the notion that you can take our initial design (Figure 12.4), which would be a minimal design for testability, and *refactor it to the open-closed* once Client₂ arrives, this seems much more realistic.

Back to the Law of Demeter

Now the Law of Demeter can be seen in a different, more practical way. Let's return to the code that violated this law and was the sort of code that suggested the law in the first place (see Figure 12.8).

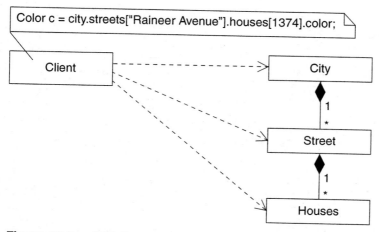

Figure 12.8   Violation of the Law of Demeter

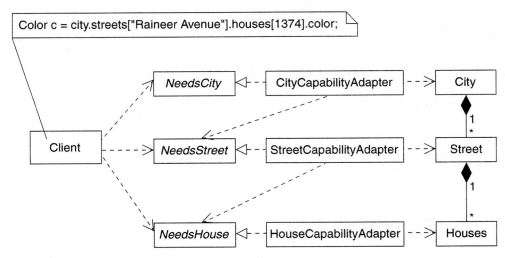

Figure 12.9   `Needs` interfaces reveal the coupling and complexity.

If we attempt to create "needs interfaces" and the adapters that separate them from capabilities, this starts to get quickly out of hand (Figure 12.9).

Note that once we try to test this, we find that the complexity and coupling in the design will increase our mocking burden in testing (see Figure 12.10).

People who start testing and mocking who have designs like this often raise a complaint after doing TDD for a while. "It seems like my job now is to create mock objects" is a common way to phrase it. Note that if we follow the Law of Demeter *and* separate needs interfaces from capabilities interfaces (see Figure 12.11), this need not happen.

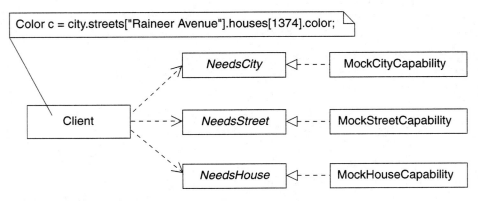

Figure 12.10   Multiple mocks needed

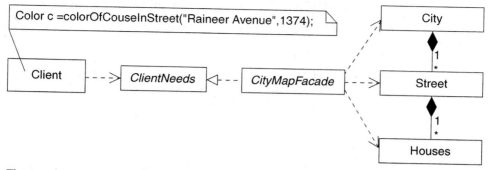

Figure 12.11   Law of Demeter with separation of needs from capabilities

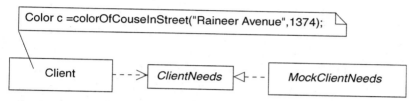

Figure 12.12   Mocking simplified because of the proper separation

This, in turn, means the mocking is limited to the single interface that reflects the needs of the `Client` (see Figure 12.12).

Summary

Interfaces are often thought to apply to what services offer, making known their capabilities. There is another type of interface: the interface that specifies what a client needs. This is the Façade Pattern or, in simple cases, the Adapter Pattern.

Focusing on the `Needs` interfaces rather than the capabilities interfaces allows for a complete encapsulation of the client's development. This has the immediate value of addressing three very common development concerns:

- "We cannot continue with our client's development because the server team does not have time for us to sit with them and finalize the interfaces."

- "We cannot continue with the client's development because the server team is not ready."

- "Now that we're trying to integrate, we have to do a lot of rework because the interface changed without our knowledge, or it doesn't behave the way we agreed it would."

Since the client is not aware of any specific server interface, it cannot couple to it and must therefore focus on what it needs the server to do for it. This is an example of Programming by Intention and adherence to the design to interfaces design rule.

A client developed that way is designed to be decoupled from any server. It makes it clear what the client needs, thus providing a check-list to the suitability of existing servers and guides the development of future servers by making the client's need explicit.

By focusing on the client's needs, the interface can return simple objects that the client understands rather than forcing the client to deal with complex server structures. This significantly simplifies the development of mocks, because all the mocks need to do is to return the simple object. No knowledge of the server structures is required, and possible changes to these structures will not affect the client.

The client becomes more cohesive as well. It is now focused on performing its duties; the details on how to communicate with a specific server are delegated to the façade or adapter.

Finally, if there is only one client and the server is tailored for it, there is no need for two interfaces. The needs are the capabilities. When a second client emerges, we will refactor to the Open-Closed principle. We will introduce a capabilities interface on the client, which initially is a copy of the needs interface but may change as the other client's needs evolve.

CHAPTER 13

When and How to Use Inheritance

The mechanism of inheritance is provided in some form by most modern programming languages. However, its improper use can lead to brittle, unnecessarily inflexible architectures that sacrifice encapsulation for little or no gain. This should not, however, lead a developer to conclude that inheritance is bad, or even that it should be used in a minimal, last-resort way. The real question is, what is inheritance good for, and when should it be used?

The Gang of Four

In their seminal book on design patterns,[1] Erich Gamma, Richard Helm, Ralph Johnson, and John Vlissides (who are often affectionately referred to as the "Gang of Four") issued several important pieces of general advice on software design. In a sense, each pattern can be thought of as, among other things, examples of following this advice when presented with a particular sort of problem or problem domain.

One such piece of advice was "favor aggregation over inheritance." Sometimes the word "aggregation" is replaced with "composition" or even "delegation," but the implication is pretty clear: Don't inherit. Instead, delegate from one object to another.

As an example, let's consider the following design decision: We have a class that represents a bank account. We'll leave out most of the implementation, but you can imagine the likely interface of such an entity (debit, credit, transfer, and so on). As part of its responsibility, however, it must apply an algorithm for calculating the interest to be paid on the account.

---

1. Gamma, Erich, Richard Helm, Robert Johnson, and John M. Vlissides. *Design Patterns: Elements of Reusable Object-Oriented Software*. Reading, MA: Addison-Wesley, 1994.

Let's say the actual algorithm varies, depending on whether this is a standard bank account or one that belongs to a "preferred customer." Most likely, the preferred customer is given a higher rate.

A fairly traditional approach would be to take the Account class and add a method to it, called calcInterest() or something similar. In the very early days of object orientation, we would have considered it reasonable to then "reuse"[2] the Account class by subclassing it as PreferredAccount and overriding the calcInterest() method with the preferred Algorithm, as shown in Figure 13.1.

This is what is often termed "direct inheritance" or "inheritance for specialization." It violates the advice of the Gang of Four. The problem is that any change one might make to Account can affect Preferred-Account, even if this is not desired, because they are coupled through inheritance.

Interestingly, the tendency to use inheritance this way comes from the original notion of open-closed. Even today we'd say, as a principle, that we would like our systems to be "open for extension but closed to modification" because we much prefer accommodating change by writing new code, rather than changing existing code. This notion of direct inheritance would seem to follow this principle, because we've created this new PreferredAccount and have left the existing code in Account alone entirely. Furthermore, if we upcast PreferredAccount

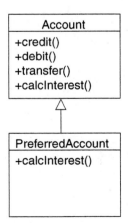

Figure 13.1   Use of direct inheritance

---

2. In fact, there are many who have said that the value of OO is precisely this form of reusing existing objects.

to `Account` wherever it is used, we won't have to change that using code either.[3]

Nevertheless, this approach can give us problems.

What if we need to make some sort of code change to `Account` that is not intended to also change `PreferredAccount`? The structure in Figure 13.1 requires care and investigation to ensure that `Preferred-Account` does not accept the unwanted change but rather overrides or shadows it. This issue of "unwanted side effects" can be even more complicated if the language makes a distinction between virtual (late-bound) and nonvirtual (early-bound) methods. Therefore, the more often inheritance is used in this way, the more difficult and dangerous it is to make changes. However, inheritance can be used in a slightly different way to avoid much of this, as shown in Figure 13.2.

The advantage here is one of control. If a developer wants to make a change that *could only* affect `StandardAccount`, the change is made to that class, and we note there is no coupling between it and `Preferred-Account`. The same is true in the reverse; a change to `Preferred-Account` *can only* affect that one single class.

If, on the other hand, the developer in fact wants to make a change that affects them both, then the change would be made to `Account`. The developer is in the driver's seat, and it's much clearer to everyone which changes will affect which entities.

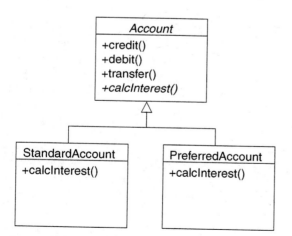

Figure 13.2   Use of abstract inheritance

---

3. It is also interesting to note that the keyword for inheritance in Java, which was invented in 1995 when this form of inheritance was quite popular, is "extends."

Still, although this is certainly better, is it good enough? If we want the effort we make to create software (which is the major cost of software in most cases) to continue to deliver value for a long time into the future, we have to pay attention not only to what a design is but also what it is likely to become.

Initial Vectors, Eventual Results

The way you begin can have a big influence on where you end up. In space flight, they call this "the initial vector," and engineers are very circumspect about it. When a spacecraft is leaving Earth's orbit and heading to the moon, for instance, if the angle of thrust is off by a fraction of a percent, you will find yourself hundreds of miles off-target by the time you reach your destination. The initial vector change is small, but the difference in the eventual result is large and significant.

Design decisions can be like this.

In other words, the larger point here is about what we do *now* versus what we will be *able to do later* and how well early solutions scale into later ones.

For example, the design in Figure 13.2 is not very dynamic. If we instantiate StandardAccount, we are committed to the calcInterest-Rate() implementation it contains. If we wanted, at runtime, to switch to the preferred algorithm, we will have to build an instance of PreferredAccount and transfer all the state that is currently held by our instance of StandardAccount into it. That means the state of StandardAccount will have to be exposed (breaking encapsulation), or we'll have to give StandardAccount a way to create an instance of PreferredAccount (and vice versa), passing the needed state through its constructor. These would be known as "cloning methods" and would couple these subtypes to each other, which we were trying to avoid in the first place.

The business rules before us *today* might say "Standard accounts never change into preferred accounts," and so we might think we're OK. Then *tomorrow* the bank holds an unexpected marketing promotion that requires this very capability. This sort of thing happens all the time.

Here's another example: In the problem currently before us, we have a single varying algorithm, the one that calculates interest. What if, at some point in the future, some other aspect of Account starts to vary?

This is an unpredictable[4] thing, and so it's certainly credible that a non-varying issue today could be a varying one tomorrow.

For instance, let's say the transfer mechanism also contains a variation. The rules have changed, and now there are two versions: immediate transfer and delayed transfer. If we try to scale the nonpreferred solution, we'd likely do something like what is shown in Figure 13.3.

All of the problems we had initially have become worse. We cannot make either varying issue dynamic (runtime-changeable) without degrading coupling or encapsulation issues, we've created more coupling through all the inheritance, and so forth.

Furthermore, given the notion of the separation of concerns, we note that the farther down the inheritance hierarchy we go, the more concerns are becoming coupled together inside single classes. When we began, Account was about one thing: modeling a bank account. Then, PreferredAccount and StandardAccount were each about two things: modeling a bank account and varying the interest calculation in a particular way. Now, all these various accounts are about three things: modeling an account, varying the interest, and varying the transfer mechanism. At each stage along the way, we are putting more concerns into a single place in each class.

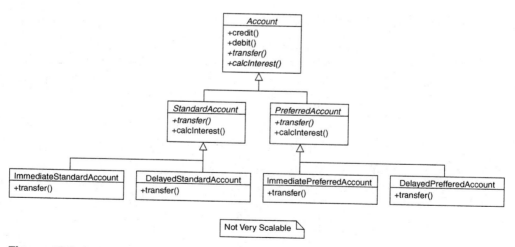

Figure 13.3   Attempting to scale the solution

---

4. Generally, most approaches to software development that require prediction are destined to fail. The world is too complex, the future is too hard to envision, and changes are too rapid for prediction to be in any sense reliable.

A Pragmatic Comment on This Example

The previous example may look contrived, but the authors have seen this result in many ways.

Imagine that we started with the delayed transfer, but now it is determined `PreferredAccounts` need to have an option to transfer immediately. It would not be unusual for someone using direct inheritance to just make a derivation of `PreferredAccount` with this type of calculation. If later we need to add this calculation for standard accounts, it will become clear that we should pull out the calculator. But consider the situation developers will find themselves in if they didn't write the code for `PreferredAccount` or if the code doesn't have a full set of tests.

In this case, there is some danger to refactoring and retesting the code, and the developer may just choose to copy and paste the calculator into a new subclass of `StandardAccount`.

It's just too easy to fall into this trap.

Favoring Delegation

The Gang of Four's advice about favoring delegation would seem to argue for something more like what is shown in Figure 13.4.

Note that the `calcInterest()` method is still implemented (not abstract), but its implementation consists merely of calling the

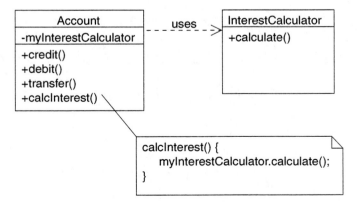

Figure 13.4   Delegating through a pointer

`calculate()` method on the service object `InterestCalculator`. This "passing the buck" behavior is what we mean by delegation.

The very act of pulling the interest calculation out of `Account` feels right, in terms of the separation of concerns, because it removes one concern from the `Account`.

Almost immediately, however, in seeking to create a variation in what we're delegating *to*, we end up putting inheritance back in again. Almost all the patterns do this in various ways, and it would seem at first glance that the Gang of Four is warning against inheritance and then using it repeatedly throughout the patterns they illustrate.

In this case, the variation is of a single algorithm and would likely be enabled through the use of the Strategy Pattern (see http://www .netobjectivesrepository.com/TheStrategyPattern), as shown in Figure 13.5.

So, what's the real recommendation? What are we favoring over what? Comparing Figures 13.2 and 13.5, we see inheritance at work in both cases, and in fact it is abstract inheritance each time.

But notice that from `Account`'s "point of view," the Gang of Four approach uses delegation to handle the variation of the interest calculation, while in the older approach inheritance is directly used on the `Account` class to achieve this variation. The difference is not whether inheritance is used; inheritance is just a mechanism, and it can be used advantageously and disadvantageously just as any mechanism can be. The difference is in what we're using inheritance *for*.

We sometimes forget that the code is not the software. It's an abstract representation that gets converted, by the compiler, into the actual software, which exists at runtime, not when we're writing it. All our work is at some abstract level, whether it is UML, code, or whatever representation we use.

Examining inheritance versus delegation at runtime can be very revealing.

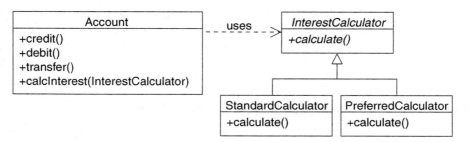

Figure 13.5   The Strategy Pattern

The Use of Inheritance versus Delegation

Let's step back and consider these two mechanisms, delegation and inheritance, in and of themselves (see Figure 13.6).

An interesting thing to note is that the relationships are in some ways more similar than they seem at first glance, when you examine them at runtime, as shown in Figure 13.7.

In Case 1, when ClassB gets loaded by the class loader and an instance is created, in fact ClassA will also load, and an instance of it will be created as well (this will happen first, in fact). This is to allow the instance of B to access the instance of A through an inherent pointer (or accessible via a keyword such as "super" or "base," and so on).

In Case 2, very similarly, an instance of ClassB will be accompanied by an instance of ClassA, which it can access via a pointer. The immediately obvious difference is how and when the instances get created and how the pointer is provided and accessed.

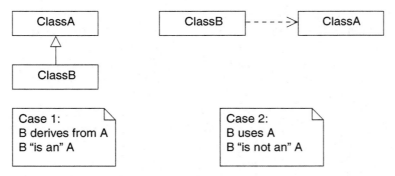

Figure 13.6   Inheritance and delegation

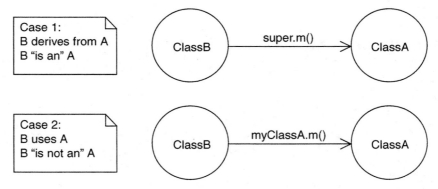

Figure 13.7   Runtime similarities

Table 13.1   Inheritance versus Delegation

Inheritance	Delegation
A reference of `ClassB` can be cast to `ClassA`. There is an implied substitutability between them.	`ClassB` and `ClassA` are distinct; there is no implication of sameness.
Any change to `ClassA` can potentially affect `ClassB`. Care must be taken to ensure that unwanted side effects in `ClassB` are overridden. Also, in some languages the issue of virtual/nonvirtual methods must be considered, as well as whether an overridden method replaces or shadows the original and whether casting can change the method implementation being bound to at runtime.	Changes to `ClassA` can affect `ClassB` only insofar as those changes propagate through `ClassB`'s interface. It is much easier to control the potential for unwanted side effects from a change, because we have stronger encapsulation.
The instance of `ClassA` that `ClassB` has access to cannot be changed after the object is created. Also, the inherent instance will always be of type `ClassA`, concretely.	The addition of a `setter()` method in `ClassB` would allow us to change the instance of `ClassA` that `ClassB` uses and in fact can give `ClassB` an instance of something other than `ClassA` (a subclass, for example), so long as it passes type-check.
The instance of `ClassA` that `ClassB` uses cannot be shared.	The instance of `ClassA` that `ClassB` uses can be shared.

These two cases, in other words, have a very similar, seemingly almost identical runtime relationship. So, why should we favor one over the other? Table 13.1 highlights some of the differences.

Uses of Inheritance

Let's examine the two options for containing our interest variation in `Account`, side by side (see Figure 13.8).

What the Gang of Four was recommending was *to use inheritance to hide variation, not to achieve reuse of code.*

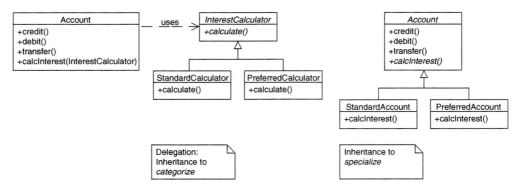

Figure 13.8 Side-by-side comparison

In their preferred solution (the one on the left), inheritance is used to create a *category*, or substitutability/pluggability, around the concept `InterestCalculator`. `InterestCalculator` itself is not "a thing" but rather "an idea." The "real" things are `StandardCalculator` and `PreferredCalculator`, which have been made interchangeable through this use of inheritance.[5]

What the Gang of Four is recommending against is the approach on the right, where `Account` (which is a "real" thing) is being *specialized* through the inheritance mechanism.

One clue for us that this is perhaps not a natural fit to the problem is in the actual code for the design on the right.

```
abstract class Account {
    public void credit() { //some implementing code }
    public void debit() { //some implementing code }
    public void transfer() { //some implementing code }
    public abstract void calcInterest();
}
```

To make this work, we've had to give `Account` an abstract method (`calcInterest()`), and therefore `Account` itself must be made abstract. But `Account` is not an abstract idea; it's a real thing. Compare this to `InterestCalculator`, which is conceptual and would therefore seem to be a more natural, logical thing to make abstract.

---

5. If you're familiar with .NET delegates, you know that a very similar end could be achieved using them, or with "interface" types in (.NET, Java, and other languages), which could have multiple implementations. The point is the pluggability; the way you get it will vary depending on the language and platform you are using and other forces operating on your decision.

This is just a clue, of course. We could artificially implement `calcInterest()` in `Account` to avoid being forced to make it abstract, but we'd be chasing our tails a bit (revisit Table 13.1 to see all the advantages we'd be giving up).

Pay particular attention to the third point in the table. If we need to change the calculation algorithm at runtime, the preferred solution is much easier on us. In the solution on the right, if we had built `StandardAccount`, the only way to switch to the preferred algorithm is to build an instance of `PreferredAccount` and *somehow transfer any state from one to the other*. This would require us to do either of the following:

- Break encapsulation on the state, so we could retrieve it from the old instance to give it to the new one

- Create a "cloning" method that allows each to remake itself as the other

This is the "dynamism problem" we encountered earlier. In the first case, we give up encapsulation; in the second, we create unnecessary coupling between these two classes.

On the other hand, if we choose to follow the Gang of Four's recommendation and use the preferred solution (the Strategy Pattern we mentioned earlier), then we need only add a method like `setCalculator(` `InterestCalculator` `aCalculator)` to the `Account` class, and *voila*, we can change the interest algorithm whenever we like, without rebuilding the `Account` object.

This also means we don't have to add that method now, if there is no such requirement. Good design often does this: We know it will be easy to add this capability later if we ever need it, and so we don't overdesign the initial solution now. See Chapter 8, Avoid Over- and Under-Design, for more details on the virtues of this.

Scalability

We saw earlier that scaling the design, where inheritance was used to specialize the `Account` object, led to ever-decreasing quality and a resulting increase in the difficulty to accommodate changes.

On the other hand, if we try to scale the Strategy Pattern solution, we can simply do what we did before: pull the new variation (transfer speed) out (see Figure 13.9).

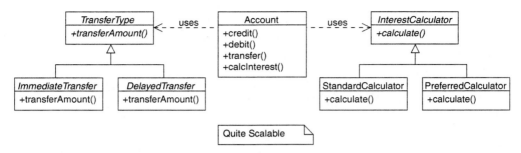

Figure 13.9 Much more scalable

Note how many aspects of the design are actually improved by this change.

For instance, many (perhaps yourself) would have argued initially that the account had too many responsibilities. Some would say that interest calculation and transfer from account to account really were always separate responsibilities, even before they started to vary. It's a fair point, but it's difficult to know how far to go[6] with the instinct to "pull stuff apart."

But note how the evolution of our design gets us to this realization, by its very nature. Our design is neither fighting us in terms of being able to accommodate change nor leading us down the primrose path in terms of overall quality. We don't have to "get everything right" in the beginning, because our initial attention to good design gives us the power to make changes efficiently, with low risk and very little waste.

Applying the Lessons from the Gang of Four to Agile Development

People often think of design patterns as a kind of design up front. One needs to remember that the design patterns came into vogue when that was mostly how you did things. However, if you explore the thought process under the patterns, you can apply that thought process to agile development just as well as you can when you are doing a big design up front—perhaps better, because the lessons of patterns tell us what to be looking at, not so much what to do.

---

6. We do have more to say on this, however. Please read Chapter 3, Define Tests Up Front, for a discussion of how tests can help us to see how far to go in separating behaviors into objects.

Let's look at the possible states you can be in at the start of the project:

- You know of multiple behaviors you need to have, and you need them right away.

- You know of multiple behaviors you need to have, but you need only the first one at the start.

- You know of only one behavior you will need to have.

Agile development tells us we should actually deal with all three of these items in a similar manner. In other words, even if we know of more than one case, we should build only the first one anyway and then go on to the second. In other words, YAGNI (You Ain't Gonna Need It) becomes YAGNIBALYW (You Are Gonna Need It But Act Like You Won't). The second case is actually how we're saying to handle the first case. The third case, of course, becomes the second case when something new comes up. Thus, we can say, in the agile world, the Gang of Four's advice to "pull out what is varying and encapsulate it" becomes "when something starts to vary, pull it out into its own class and encapsulate it." This complements the ideas expressed in Chapter 11, Refactor to the Open-Closed.

This approach allows us to follow another powerful principle of software design: A class should have only one reason to vary. Although this too has often been used as a principle for up-front designs, we can now see that it tells us to extract variation from classes as it starts to occur.

Testing Issues

We have another chapter on testing, but it's interesting to note here that the use of inheritance in the way the Gang of Four is recommending plays well into testing scenarios.

In short, our definition of a good test is one that fails for a single, reliable reason. Our definition of a good test suite is one where a single change or bug can only ever break a single test. These are ideals, of course, and cannot be perfectly achieved, but it is always our goal to get as close as we can. Taken together, these bits of guidance make our tests more useful and keep our suites from become maintenance problems in and of themselves.

We note that the use of a mock object in our Strategy Pattern achieves these goals perfectly (see Figure 13.10).

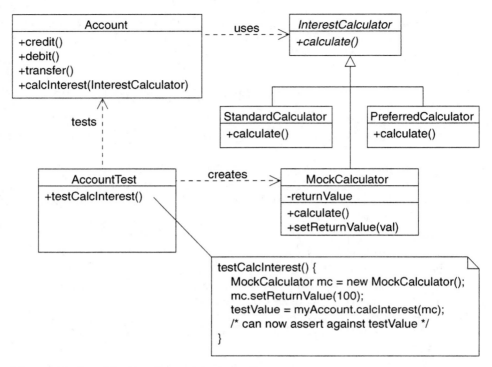

Figure 13.10   Mocking for testing separation

The test for `Account` would instantiate `MockCalculator` and hold it as `MockCalculator`, which gives it access to `setReturnValue()` and any other for-testing-only method we care to add (there are many possibilities; this is an intentionally simple example). In handing it to `Account`, however, note it will be upcast to `InterestCalculator` (because of the parameter type), and thus `Account` cannot become coupled to the testing methods, or the existence of the mock at all.

Testing each calculator requires a single test per implementation, which can fail only if the calculator is broken or changed.

Testing `Account` is done in the context of `MockCalculator`, so breaking or changing either of the "real" calculators will not cause the test for `Account` to fail. The `Account` test can fail only if `Account` is actually broken or changed.

There's More

This example is simple, intentionally so to make the point clear. Many, many more examples are available that show how inheritance can be used in this preferred way (to create categories for pluggability).

They are all design patterns.

Visit http://www.netobjectives.com/PatternRepository for more examples of how inheritance can be used to create pluggability and dynamism.

PART IV

Appendixes

APPENDIX A

Overview of the Unified Modeling Language (UML)

This appendix[1] gives a brief overview of the Unified Modeling Language (UML), which is the modeling language of the object-oriented community. If you do not already know the UML, this appendix will give you the minimal understanding you will need to be able to read the diagrams contained in this book.

- *We describe what the UML is and why to use it.*
- *We discuss the UML diagrams that are essential to this book.*
  - *The class diagram*
  - *The sequence diagram*

What Is the UML?

The UML is a visual language (meaning a drawing notation with semantics) used to create models of programs. By models of programs, we mean a diagrammatic representation of the programs in which one can see the relationships between the objects in the code.

The UML has several different diagrams—some for analysis, others for design, and still others for implementation (or more accurately, for the deployment). For the purposes of reading this book, you will need to understand class and sequence diagrams, so we will focus specifically on them.

---

1. This appendix is based on Chapter 2 of *Design Patterns Explained* by Shalloway and Trott.

Why Use the UML?

There are three reasons to use the UML:

- **Principally for communication.** The UML is used primarily for communication—with oneself, with team members, and with our customers. Poor requirements (incomplete, inaccurate, or misunderstood) are ubiquitous in the field of software development. The UML gives us tools to elicit better requirements.

- **For clarity.** The UML gives a way to help determine whether our understanding of the system is the same as others' understanding of it. Because systems are complex and have different types of information that must be conveyed, it offers different diagrams specializing in the different types of information.

- **For precision.** One easy way to see the value of the UML is to recall your last several design reviews. If you have ever been in a review where someone starts talking about his or her code and describes it without a modeling language like the UML, almost certainly his or her talk was both confusing and much longer than necessary. Not only is the UML a better way of describing object-oriented designs, but it also forces designers to think through the relationships between classes in his or her approach (since they must be written down).

The Class Diagram

The most basic of UML diagrams is the class diagram. It both describes classes and shows the relationships among them. The types of relationships that are possible are the following:

- When one class is a "kind of" another class: the "is-a" relationship
- When there are associations between two classes
  - One class "contains" another class: the "has-a" relationship
  - One class "uses" another class: the "uses-a" relationship
- One class "creates" another class

There are variations on these themes. For example, to say something contains something else can mean the following:

- The contained item is part of the containing item (like an engine in a car).

- The containing item holds a collection of things that can exist on their own (like airplanes at an airport).

The first example is called *composition*, while the second is called *aggregation*.

Figure A.1 illustrates several important things. First, each rectangle represents a class. In the UML, we can represent up to three aspects of a class:

- The name of the class

- The data members of the class

- The methods (functions) of the class

There are three different ways of showing this information.

- The *leftmost rectangle* shows just the class's name. We use this type of class representation when more detailed information is not needed.

- The *middle rectangle* shows both the name and the methods of the class. In this case, Square has the method display(). The plus sign (+) in front of display() (the name of the method) means that this method is public—that is, objects other than objects of this class can call it.

- The *rightmost rectangle* shows what we had before (the name and methods of the class) as well as data members of the class. In this case, the minus sign (−) before the data member length (which is of type double) indicates that this data member's value is private, which means it is unavailable to anything other than the object to which it belongs.

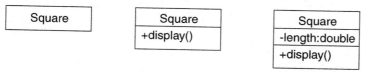

Figure A.1   Three variations on the class diagram

UML Notation for Access

You can control the accessibility of a class's data and method members. You can use the UML to notate which accessibility you want each member to have. The three most common types of accessibility available in most object-oriented languages are as follows.

- **Public.** Notated with a plus sign (+).This means all objects can access this data or method.

- **Protected.** Notated with a number sign (#). This means only this class and all of its derivations (including derivations from its derivations) can access this data or method.

- **Private.** Notated with a minus sign (–). This means that only methods of this class can access this data or method. (Note: Most languages further restrict this to the particular instance of the class in question.)

Class Diagrams Also Show Relationships

Class diagrams can also show relationships between different classes. Figure A.2 shows the relationship between the Shape class and several classes that derive from it.

Figure A.2 represents several things. First, the arrowhead under the Shape class means that those classes pointing to Shape derive from Shape. Furthermore, Shape is *italicized*, which means it is an abstract class. An abstract class is a class that is used to define the interface[2] for the classes that derive from it as well as being a place to put any common

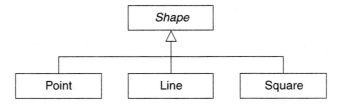

Figure A.2   The class diagram showing an "is-a" relationship

---

2. It is unfortunate that the term "interface" really has two meanings these days: It means "the defined way to communicate with an entity," but it is also a key word in many languages to mean "a type that defines an interface only." We can use the interface type or an abstract class type to define an interface in the first sense of the word.

data and methods of these derived classes. An interface can be thought of as an abstract class that has no common data or methods—it merely serves as a way of defining the methods of the classes that implement it.

Showing the "has-a" Relationship

There are actually two different kinds of "has-a" relationships. One object can have another object where the contained object is part of the containing object—or not. In Figure A.3, we show Airport "having" Aircraft. Aircraft are not part of Airport, but we can still say Airport has them. This type of relationship is called *aggregation*.

In this diagram, we also show that an Aircraft is either a Jet or a Helicopter. One can see that Aircraft is an abstract class or an interface because its name is shown in italics. That means that an Airport will have either Jet or Helicopter but can treat them the same (as Aircraft). The open (unfilled) diamond on the right of the Airport class indicates the aggregation relationship.

An airport is still an airport even if no aircraft are present. Also other airports may "have" a given aircraft at different times. This is a good example of the aggregation relationship.

The other type of "has-a" relationship is where the containment means the contained object is part of the containing object. This type of relationship is also called *composition*.

A Car is really not a complete thing without an Engine. Where the car goes, so goes the engine, and a given engine is bound to a given car. This is an example of a composition relationship.

Composition and Uses

Figure A.4 also shows that a Car uses a GasStation. The "uses" relationship is depicted by a dashed line with an arrow. This is also called a "dependency relationship."

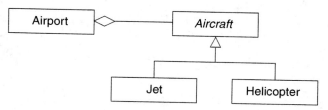

Figure A.3   The class diagram showing the "has-a" relationship called "aggregation"

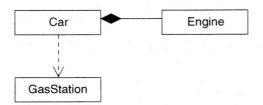

Figure A.4   The class diagram showing the "has-a" relationship called "composition" and also a "uses" relationship to GasStation

Composition versus Aggregation

Both composition and aggregation involve one object containing one or more objects. Composition, however, implies the contained object is part of the containing object, whereas aggregation means the contained objects are a collection of entities. We can consider composition to be an unshared association, with the contained object's lifetime being controlled by its containing object. The appropriate use of constructors and destructors is useful here to help facilitate object creation and destruction. This distinction is more important in unmanaged code (like C++) because in composition the destruction of the containing object should be accompanied by the destruction of the contained object(s), whereas in aggregation it should not.

If one is working in managed code (like Java or C#), this issue is a matter for the garbage collector anyway.

Notes in the UML

In Figure A.5, there is a new symbol: the note. The box containing the message "open diamond means aggregation" is a note. They are meant to look like pieces of paper with the right corner folded back. You often see them with a line connecting them to a particular symbol indicating they relate just to that symbol.

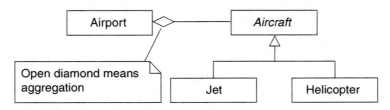

Figure A.5   A class diagram with a note included

Indicating the Number of Things Another Object Has

Class diagrams show the relationships among classes. With composition and aggregation, however, the relationship is more specifically about objects of that type of class. For example, it is true `Airports` have `Aircraft`, but more specifically, specific airports have specific aircraft. The question may arise—"How many aircraft does an airport have?" This is called the *cardinality* of the relationship. This is shown in Figures A-6 and A-7.

Figure A.6 tells us that when an `Airport` exists, it has from 0 to any number (represented by an asterisk here, but sometimes by the letter "n") of `Aircraft`. The "0..1" on the `Airport` side means that when an `Aircraft` exists, it can be contained by either 0 or 1 `Airport` (it may be in the air). However, an aircraft cannot be contained by more than one `Airport` at any given point in time.

Figure A.7 tells us that when a `Car` exists, it has either four or five wheels (it may or may not have a spare). Wheels are on exactly one car. We have heard some people assume no specification of cardinality assumes that there is one object. That may not be true and should not be assumed. If cardinality is not specified, there is no assumption made as to how many objects there are.

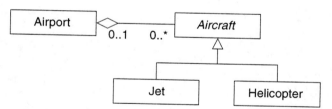

Figure A.6   The cardinality of the `Airport-Aircraft` relationship

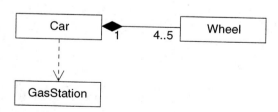

Figure A.7   The cardinality of the `Car-Tire` relationship

Dashes Show Dependence

As before, the dashed line between `Car` and `GasStation` in Figure A.7 shows that there is a dependency between the two. The UML uses a dashed arrow to indicate semantic relationships (meanings) between two model elements.

Sequence Diagram

Class diagrams show static (design-time) relationships between classes. In other words, they do not show us any activity. Although very useful, sometimes we need to show how the objects instantiated from these classes actually work together (at runtime).

The UML diagrams that show how objects interact with each other are called "interaction diagrams." The most common type of interaction diagram is the sequence diagram, such as shown in Figure A.8.

For example, in Figure A.8, at the top of the diagram you can see that `Main` sends a "get shapes" message to the `ShapeFactory` object (which isn't named). After being asked to "get shapes," the `ShapeFactory` does the following:

- Instantiates a collection
- Instantiates a square
- Adds the square to the collection
- Instantiates a circle
- Adds the circle to the collection
- Returns the collection to the calling routine (the `Main`)

We read the rest of the diagram in this top-down fashion to see the rest of the action. This diagram is called a sequence diagram because it depicts the sequence of operations.

Object:Class Notation

In some UML diagrams, you want to refer to an object with the class from which it is derived. This is done by connecting them with a colon. Figure A.8 shows `shape1:Square` refers to the `shape1` object, which is instantiated from the `Square` class.

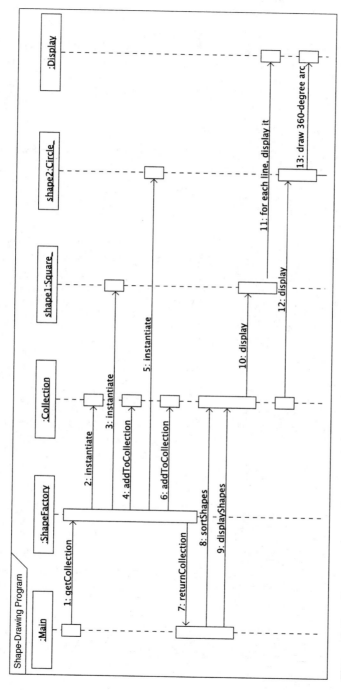

Figure A.8   Sequence diagram for a shape-drawing program

Summary

The purpose of the UML is both to flesh out your designs and to communicate them. Do not worry so much about creating diagrams the "right" way. Think about the best way to communicate the concepts in your design. In other words,

- If you think something needs to be said, use a note to say it.

- If you aren't sure about an icon or a symbol and you have to look it up to find out its meaning, include a note to explain it since others may be unclear about its meaning, too.

- Go for clarity.

Of course, this means you should not use the UML in nonstandard ways; that does not communicate properly either. Just consider what you are trying to communicate as your draw your diagrams.

For a more complete discussion of the UML, the authors recommend Martin Fowler's excellent *UML Distilled*, which not only focuses on the aspects of the UML that are most commonly used but also provides much wisdom about effective modeling using this tool.

APPENDIX B

Code Qualities

Good design, up-front testing, and practices such as Programming by Intention and encapsulating constructors (all topics covered in this book) are things we think will help you create better software. At the root of all these practices, principles, and disciplines are the qualities of code that make software easier to change, debug, enhance, and tune. If you've read any of the books we produce, you are familiar with these, because they are always an important part of any engineering practice we promote.

This is meant to be a summary for those who have not read our books, or a review if desired.

For each quality, we will describe it generally, mention any principles that it adheres to or promotes, suggest practices that will help you enhance the quality, note any indicators that might tell you that your code is lacking in the quality (pathologies), and note any testing issues that might help you to see how well you are achieving them.

First, however, we'll start with an analogy.

Christmas-Tree Lights: An Analogy

When the holidays come, many of us head up to the attic to retrieve the boxes of decorations that have been waiting all year to be called into service again. In my (Scott's) family, we put up and decorate a Christmas tree each year, but I suspect Hanukah and Kwanza and other holidays have their festive ornaments, too, and probably electric lights are involved.

One thing I'll do this year, as I do every year, is lay out the strings of lights on my coffee table and plug them all in, to see whether any of them fails to illuminate.

My parents did this, too, but they had a different kind of light set than I do. The lights in those days used a screw-in connection, like a typical light bulb, and were wired in simple series. Because of this, if one light burned out, the entire string would go dark, and you'd have to check each bulb to find the bad one. Luckily, this did not happen that often, and we used the same strings for years on end.

Modern strings, the ones I have, are usually different. They have a simple, push-in connection for each bulb, and the design includes a bypass mechanism in the sockets such that even if one bulb goes out, the rest of the string will stay lit, making the bad bulb obvious. It was a good idea, because the bulbs are smaller and there are many more of them (my strings have 150 lights per string; my father's had maybe 15).

So, with this modern design, the entire string should never go out. In theory.

I'm often reminded of a quote Al likes to use in class, alternately attributed to Yogi Berra or Jan L. A. van de Snepscheut: "In theory, there is no difference between theory and practice. But, in practice, there is." I almost always have a light string or two that is dead.

Why? There are a number of possibilities. These modern strings are also made much more cheaply than the ones my parents owned. Sometimes, because of the simple, push-in connection and the soft plastic of the socket, a bulb gets in only partway or gets twisted slightly. Sometimes the cheap little bent-back wires sticking out of the bulb, which are supposed to make the connection, will break or bend the wrong way. The wiring between the sockets is also lower quality and can develop breaks. The pass-through mechanisms in the sockets are also cheaply made and can fail. The plug at the end of the cord, cheap plastic again, can fail, or the fuse inside it could be blown.

What do I do with such a string? The same thing I suspect you do; I throw it away. Finding the problem would take too much of my time to be worth it, especially given how low in cost a new string will be anyway. I might check the fuse, but beyond that, I toss it. Wouldn't you like to do that with some of the legacy systems you deal with?

So, this is the first part of my analogy: Even a "better" design idea will not produce greater value if quality is allowed to suffer. You can code an Abstract Factory as a single class with a set of methods that each has a switch-case statement, all based on a control variable, but the fact that you "used a pattern" does not mean your code is good quality (or vice versa). This can really matter when you have to debug, enhance, or otherwise maintain it—in other words, pretty much always.

But let's take this further. Each of these failure possibilities is a lesson.

Each socket is dependent on the wiring that leads to it and away from it and upon the proper behavior of each socket those wires connect to, to the sockets they are connected to, and so on. This *coupling* means that a failure of anything in any socket can affect other sockets, causing them to fail. And, all sockets are coupled to the plug, the fuse inside the plug, the electrical system in your house, and so on.

Each socket has a number of reasons to fail because each one actually does multiple things. It supplies energy to the bulb, it ensures the bulb is properly positioned in the socket to receive it, and it passes energy through to the next socket. This lack of *cohesion* in the sockets means it is hard for us to know which of these aspects is failing when the string goes dark.

Finally, worst of all, every socket is a repeat of every other socket. This *redundancy* of design means that it is impossible to know which one of them is failing, since they are all candidates for all the same failures. What if two or more of them are failing? It will not be enough to swap out each bulb in turn, because if many of them have badly bent wires or many are twisted in their sockets...what a nightmare.

What if I had a device that I could plug my string of lights into that, with a simple press of a button, would test every individual aspect of my string and tell me exactly what was wrong immediately? That would be wonderful! I'd never throw a string away again. This is very much like an automated suite of unit tests.

But, we'll probably never have such a device. The manifold coupling, weak cohesion, and multiple redundancies would make it too hard to achieve. That's why legacy code almost never has tests. The lack of quality usually makes them too difficult to implement.

We can follow this analogy yet further.

Let's say I discard and replace any bad strings and so now all my strings light properly. Now I put them all on the tree and then add ornaments, garland, tinsel, popcorn strings, and so on...beautiful!

On Christmas Eve, just as my friends and extended family are about to arrive for our celebration, one string in the middle of the tree goes out. Big dark spot, right in front. It looks terrible and will spoil things.

Now, throwing it away and replacing it is not an option; it has become too entangled with everything else on the tree. That laborious socket-by-socket, wire-by-wire, arduous inspection of the string (which was not worth it to me before) is now my only option. It will actually be made *more* difficult (and much more unpleasant) because the string is in place on the tree. It'll be several hours of pine needles in my eyes and broken ornaments before I solve this problem, if I ever do. Everyone is due in four hours, the deadline approaches, and Andrea wants to know when I'll have it working and when I'll be available to help with the hors d'oeuvres.

Our software, and its quality, does not affect us alone, because increasingly software is being created from other software; we create services that may well end up in the center of a system or systems that we did not anticipate. We depend upon the good work of other developers, and they depend on us.

Quality is worth it; if we want to be able to create software with persistent value rather than systems, we simply rewrite and throw away on a regular basis. As software becomes more important in the world and as there is more and more of it to enhance and maintain, focus on quality becomes increasingly important.

Good-quality software is understandable, is testable, and can be changed to meet the ever-changing needs of business and individuals. It is a timeless way of building, so to speak.

Now, if you'll excuse me, I need to get the ladder and climb into the attic.

Cohesion

Description

All the elements in a class or method are related to each other. Classes and methods do not contain any unrelated or "red herring" elements.

Poor cohesion is termed "weak." Good cohesion is termed "strong."

Cohesion is fractal; it can be considered at many levels: statement, method, class, namespace, package, subsystem, application, and so on. In design, we find it most valuable to concentrate on the cohesion of classes and methods primarily.

A "strongly" cohesive class is one where all of its internal aspects (state, functions, relationships, and so on) are about fulfilling the same, single "responsibility."

A "strongly" cohesive method is about implementing a single "functional" aspect of a class's responsibility.

Principles

- Single Responsibility principle
- Separation of concerns

Practices

- Programming by Intention
- Up-front testing
- Commonality-Variability Analysis

Pathologies

- **Large classes.** A large class may be large because it has more than one responsibility.

- **Long methods.** A long method may contain more than one function.

- **Difficulty naming.** It is hard to give a class or method an intention-revealing name if it does many unrelated things. Or, such a name would have to be very long, perhaps containing underscores or "ands." This is an indication that the entity may not be strongly cohesive.

Indications in Testing

- **Large tests.** If a class contains more than one responsibility, the test for that class must test them all, and all of their possible combinations, because of possible side effects. This often results in tests that are significantly longer than the classes they test. When each responsibility of the system is in a separate class, then we know that side effects are much more limited, and thus the classes can largely be tested in isolation from one another. These tests tend to be smaller and simpler.

- **Tests that fail for multiple reasons.** Another way to express that a class is cohesive is to say there is only one reason it could fail. Tests reveal this insofar as they will fail for any reason that the class can fail.

Coupling

Description

The dependencies between a given entity and other entities are logical, obvious, and minimal.

Good coupling is often termed "loose," but we prefer "intentional." Bad coupling is often termed "tight," but we prefer "accidental."

There are many kinds of coupling, but the following are the primary types that concern us:

- **Identity coupling.** This exists when one type couples to the existence of another type. Usually this occurs when ClassA has a member of type ClassB, takes a parameter of type ClassB in one of its methods, or returns a reference of type ClassB from one of its methods. If ClassA will not compile when ClassB is removed from the system (yielding a "class not found" error), this indicates identity coupling.

- **Representational coupling.** This exists when one type couples to the interface of another type. If ClassA will not compile when the public interface of ClassB is changed, this indicates representational coupling.

- **Inheritance coupling.** This is the coupling that is created between a derived class and its base class. A subclass may be changed when its base type is changed, and so this must be taken into account when some changes are made. When inheritance is used extensively throughout a design, especially when it is allowed to cascade in large hierarchies, the inheritance coupling can get out of hand.

- **Subclass coupling.** This exists when one type is coupled to the fact that another type is polymorphic, not simple. Classes that have no subclass coupling have no special indications in their code that a class they depend upon is either concrete or really one of many classes that have been upcast to an abstract type. When subclass coupling is present, a class depending on subtype X will have to change when it must depend instead on subtype Y.

Principles

- The Open-Closed principle

Practices

- Encapsulate by policy, reveal by need
- Design to interfaces
- Using inheritance for pluggability, not specialization
- Up-front testing

Pathologies

- Unexpected side effects when changes are made

Indications in Testing

- **Slow, complex tests.** These indicate that a class may have many dependencies that must be present when the class is tested. Instantiating these dependencies can take time and thus slow down the testing. Also, direct coupling to external entities, such as databases and user interfaces, can also require actions that slow the tests (populating the database with test data, for example).

- **Large test fixtures.** These also can indicate this coupling. The "fixture" of a test consists of all the instances it must create to accomplish the testing. If there are many objects, this may indicate more coupling in the system than is desirable.

Redundancy

Description

Anything that could change (read: *anything*) should be in a single place in the system, including the following:

- State
- Function
- Rules
- Object creation (memory allocation)
- Relationships

Principles

- One rule, one place
- Don't Repeat Yourself (DRY)
- Shalloway's law

Practices

- Refactor redundancies immediately.
- When two entities require the same service, state, relationship, behavior, and so on, design for any number. Consider 0 and 1 to be unique, whereas 2 represents all other numbers.
- Up-front testing

Pathologies

- Duplication in client objects
- When searching for a bug or integration point, uncertainty that you can stop once you find it

Indications in Testing

- **Duplication in tests.** Often issues that are subtly redundant in the production code are more obviously redundant in tests, and so testing represents an additional opportunity to notice them. The upshot can be this: If a test has redundancies that cannot be refactored out, then this probably indicates there are redundancies in the system.

Encapsulation

Description

While encapsulation is often defined as "data hiding," in truth it is the hiding of anything. Any time one part of the system becomes shielded from another part of the system, we consider it encapsulated. This can include the following:

- Data/state
- Behavior
- Type
- Construction/memory allocation
- The number of service objects being used
- The order that multiple service objects are used in
- Interface
- Entity
- Subsystems

Anything that can be encapsulated without impeding the behavior of the system should be, because this will fundamentally affect the previous qualities listed in this appendix.

- **Cohesion.** The more cohesive entities are, the more encapsulation is possible. A single class with all behavior in it would be very weakly cohesive, and there would be essentially no encapsulation ("private" means nothing within a class). Therefore, the desire to encapsulate requires cohesive design.
- **Coupling.** That which cannot be seen cannot be coupled to.
- **Redundancy.** The desire to eliminate redundancy often requires the use of reusable service objects. These objects add encapsulation that is not present when clients contain service code within them.

Principles

- Encapsulate all variation

Practices

- Encapsulate by policy; reveal only with a clearly defined need

Pathologies

- Unmaintainable systems. Because encapsulation relates to the core qualities of maintainable code, severely unmaintainable systems usually lack fundamental encapsulation.

Indications in Testing

- **Coarse-grained tests.** These tell you very little when they fail (often termed "pinning tests"); they are usually the only tests that can be written for a system that has very poor encapsulation. Attempting to test all the variations in a system where side effects are unknown and unpredictable is usually too difficult to be attempted, so developers or testers will record the output of the system given a set of inputs and test against this overall expectation. Such a test can fail if *anything* in the system is broken, and therefore when they fail, they do not give any indication as to what is wrong. In refactoring legacy systems, we often start by adding these tests, which are better than nothing, and then by improving them as the encapsulation is added to the system.

APPENDIX C

Encapsulating Primitives

Encapsulation in object-oriented programming is often interpreted as making sure classes do not expose their implementation. You can go beyond this interpretation and encapsulate all the concepts in your program. Encapsulating implementations in abstract data types provides benefits in code readability, testability, and quality.[1]

Encapsulating Primitives in Abstract Data Types

Let's start with a typical method.

```
double getDiscount(double orderTotal) {}
```

With encapsulation, we are not concerned with the implementation of `getDiscount()`, only its interface: the signature of the method. Looking just at the signature, it's easy to envision what the method does. It receives the total for an order and returns the discount. However, it's harder to determine what the meaning is of that discount. Is it in percent, or is it in dollars or another currency? Now the method could be named.

```
double getDiscountPercentage(double orderTotal) {}
```

```
//or
```

```
double getDiscountAmount(double orderTotal) {}
```

---

1. Pugh, Ken. *Prefactoring: Extreme Abstraction, Extreme Separation, Extreme Readability.* Sebastopol, CA: O'Reilly Media, 2005.

If you use an abstract data type, such as `Percentage` or `Dollar`, the intent of the method can be clearer. The following is an example:

```
Percentage getDiscount(double orderTotal) {}
Dollar getDiscount(double orderTotal) {}
```

Of course, as soon as you have a `Dollar` data type, you can and should use it everywhere. So, the methods would look like the following:

```
Percentage getDiscount(Dollar orderTotal) {}
Dollar getDiscount(Dollar orderTotal) {}
```

Principles

Several principles underlie the use of abstract data types (ADTs). Gerry Weinberg states that one should not throw away information. If you already know that `orderTotal` is a dollar, then declaring it as a double throws away that information. Lean software development states you should defer decisions to the last responsible moment. If you declare `orderTotal` as a `Dollar`, you can defer any decision to use a particular implementation such as a double, a long, or a BigInteger.

The amount of effort to transform code from one form to another is not always the same in both directions. You can change the name of a method and its references back and forth by performing a search and replace or using a refactoring tool. So, switching `getDiscount()` to `getDiscountPercentage()` or back is easy. Of course, if you attempt to switch `getDiscountPercentage()` to `getDiscount()`, you will get a "method already defined" compile error if a `getDiscount()` method already exists in the same scope.

On the other hand, the transformations from `Dollar` to double and back again are not equal. A search and replace can change `Dollar` to double everywhere. To reverse the transformation, you can search for double. But you need to examine every instance to see whether `Dollar` is the appropriate replacement.

Having an ADT can help you create more cohesive classes. If you need to round off a dollar, it is fairly apparent that the rounding implementation belongs in the `Dollar` class, rather than in the method that is using `Dollar`.

Narrow the Contract

An abstract data type can narrow the contract for a concept and often simplify the testing required. For example, an int can contain values ranging from negative 2 billion to positive 2 billion. Declaring outsideTemperature to be an int suggests that it could take on any value within that range. For example, the method

```
void adjustAirConditioning(int outsideTemperature){}
```

should be tested for the limits in the realm of possibility for a particular application. You normally do this by testing for values just within and just outside the low and high limit, a total of four tests. If you create a Fahrenheit type, you need to test that class for the limits. But any method to which you pass a Fahrenheit object, such as

```
void adjustAirConditioning(Fahrenheit outsideTemperature){}
```

need only be tested at the limits of Fahrenheit. The method cannot be tested for values beyond the limits, since it is impossible to pass it those values.

The narrowing of the contract also applies to available operations on a data type. An int or a double has a plethora of operations that can be performed on them (arithmetic, logical, and so on). Most ADTs have a very limited set of functions. Limiting the operations to just those required provides further delineation of the meaning of that type.

If you need to perform operations on abstract data types, you can either overload operators in languages that permit it or create named methods in languages such as Java that do not have overloaded operators. Using named methods, you might create the following:

```
class Dollar {
   Dollar add(Dollar other);
   Dollar subtract(Dollar other);
   Percentage divide(Dollar other, RoundOff rounding);
   Dollar multiply(Percentage other, RoundOff rounding);
}
```

The auxiliary enum RoundOff would have values such as RoundUp and RoundDown.

Expanding Abstract Data Types

You can readily change from simple measurements to a more complex data type. For example, you can change `Dollar` to `Currency` or `Fahrenheit` to `Temperature`. In either case, you add an additional attribute to the class that identifies the measurement (for example, `Dollar`, `Euro`, `Yen`, or `Fahrenheit`, `Celsius`). The class becomes the focus for conversion between the different measures. The following is an example:

```
enum TemperatureMeasure {Fahrenheit, Celsius};
class Temperature{
  Temperature getAs(TemperatureMeasure tm) {}
  Boolean greaterThan(Temperature other) {}
}
```

`getAs(TemperatureMeasure tm)` either returns the temperature if it is already in the requested units or converts it if it is not. `Boolean greaterThan(Temperature other)` compares the two temperatures, regardless of their measure.

You can make abstract data types for variables that might typically be declared as strings. Strings are classes in almost every language. By having an ADT, you can narrow the contract for what the string can contain, as well as having a cohesive class that also incorporates formatting. For example, you can have the following:

```
PhoneNumber phoneNumber;
ZIPCode zipCode;
EmailAddress emailAddress;
```

Each of those classes can ensure that the objects contain only a valid formatted series of characters. You could also have classes that represented more general concepts. For example, you might have the following:

```
StringWithoutSpecialChars name;
StringWithoutSpecialChars street;
```

The `StringWithoutSpecialChars` class would ensure that no special characters (such as { or & or =) could be inside an object.

Use Text as External Values

You have to be able to read the output of a program. You need to be able to input values into a program without specifying 1s and 0s. A program may need to communicate values with a program written in a different language or running on a different machine with a different processor or operating system. Text is the common mode of communication. However, values should be converted from text to the abstract data type on input from the user interface or another system as soon as possible. The abstract data type being sent to the display or another system should be converted to text at the last possible moment. This decouples the program's internal manifestation from the external representation of data.

For example, a user interface might look like Figure C.1.

Now the submit button is clicked. The text is transmitted either directly to a program or via an HTTP link to another system. For example, the HTTP might look like the following:

```
http:// samscdrental.com/enter_user?name=SAM+phone_number
=123-456-789+zipcode=12345+email=ken.pugh@netobjectives.com
```

In either case, the receiving program should convert the text to an internal representation as soon as it receives it. In this example, the representation could appear as follows:

```
class UserEntry{
   StringWithoutSpecialChars name;
   PhoneNumber phoneNumber;
   ZIPCode zipCode;
   EmailAddress emailAddress;
}
```

Figure C.1   Typical user interface

If there is an error in conversion, it is immediately reported, and no further processing takes place on the input. Now each of the fields has the proper format. Further validation of values, such as ensuring that the emailAddress is a real one, can then take place. This would involve further processing such as sending a mail message and checking for a response.

Here's another example of how separating the external representation from internal representation gives separation of concerns. If you used the value of a character directly to determine an action to perform, you might have a method that looks like the following:

```
void someMethod(char typeCharacter){
  switch(typeCharacter){
    case 'A':
      doSomething();
      break;

    case 'B':
      doSomethingElse();
      break;

    //...
    default:
      throw BadInputCharacter("SomeMethod   "
        + Character);
  }
```

The preceding method does two things: It verifies that typeCharacter is a valid character and performs the corresponding operation. We could break that method into two methods.

```
enum CharacterState {AState, BState, ....};
CharacterState determineState(char typeCharacter) {
  switch(typeCharacter){
    case 'A':
      return AState;
    case 'B':
      return BState;
    default:
      throw new BadInputCharacter("determineState   "
        + Character);
  }
}
void actOnState(CharacterState state){
  switch(state){
    case AState:
      doSomething();
```

```
      break;
   case BState:
     do SomethingElse();
     break;
  }
}
```

Now `determineState()` and `actOnState()` each has a simple purpose. The first determines what state the input character represents and whether there is a valid state for it. The second performs an action based on that state. Now the first method could easily be converted to a table form or to one that does a database lookup. The second method would not have to change regardless of the change in the first method.

Enumerations Instead of Magic Values

Enumerations are the way to encapsulate magic values, such as those used to designate different choices, such as economy class, business class, and first class or any other fixed set of values. Instead of using either numbers (for example, `EconomyClass` is 1, `BusinessClass` is 2, and `FirstClass` is 3) or letters (for example, `EconomyClass` is E, `BusinessClass` is B, and `FirstClass` is F), in almost any language you can declare an enumeration.

```
enum TicketClass {EconomyClass, BusinessClass, FirstClass};
```

The compiler assigns unique values to each of the three symbols. In many languages, you can designate your own values for each of the symbols. That's a shortcut that could be used, but it mixes external representation in with the abstraction. If you need to convert between external representation and the internal value, you can either make up a conversion class or create class methods. The following is an example:

```
class TicketClassHelper {
  static TicketClass parse(String input);
  // Throws argument exception if unable to convert
  static String toString(TicketClass in);
  static String [] getTicketClassStrings();
}
```

The method `parse(String input)` converts a string to a Ticket-Class value; `toString(TicketClass  in)` does the reverse; and `getTicketClassStrings()` gives an array of strings corresponding to every value in `TicketClass`. You can use this array to create a drop-down list in your user interface.[2]

Disadvantages

There are disadvantages to using abstract data types for all concepts. It does increase the number of classes in a program. In some languages, such as Java, there may be a performance penalty, since primitives are passed by value on the stack and objects must be allocated and deallocated. In other languages, such as C++ and C#, the abstract data types can be passed by value on the stack.

If there are numerous combinations of operations (such as `Dollar` divided by `Percentage` and `Fahrenheit` multiplied by `Percentage`), then there will be many overloaded operations that will need to be created. This may be the case more frequently in scientific applications than in business applications. In languages that do not support overloaded operators, the method names for the operations will lengthen the source code.[3]

What Could Abstract Data Types Save?

What could be the cost of not using abstract data types? On September 23, 1999, NASA lost the Mars Climate Orbiter at a cost of $125 million. One engineering team used metric units while another used English units for a key spacecraft operation. However, instead of storing them in meter and feet, they were stored in something like double, thereby losing the information that would have discovered the error.

---

2. You might also have a byIndex(int index) that returns the TicketClass value corresponding to the location in the array of strings. You can use the selected index from the drop-down list to get the corresponding TicketClass value.
3. In the current version of C# and the .NET runtime, structs up to 16 bytes long are allocated on the stack and passed by value. An abstract data type declared as a struct contains just the same primitive that would have been used without encapsulation and takes no more time to pass than the primitive.

Summary

Abstract data types can make your code more readable and testable. They encapsulate the representation of a concept and allow the implementation to easily change.

ADTs classes provide a common location for conversions between external representations and internal representations of value. This common location can help ensure that input representations are properly formatted.

In some languages, extensive use of ADTs may cause performance issues. In languages that do not allow operator overloading, there can be an increase in the size of the code because of longer method names.

Index

A

Abstract classes
   creating one-to-one relation-
      ship, 52
   definition of, 194–195
   in encapsulation of object type,
      65
   interfaces as, 81–82, 195
   reducing redundancy using, 48
   specification giving better
      understanding of, 134
   in Variability Analysis, 133–134
Abstract data types (ADTs)
   cost of not using, 219
   disadvantages of, 219
   encapsulating primitives in,
      211–212
   enumerations instead of magic
      values, 218–219
   expanding, 214
   narrowing contract for concept,
      213
   underlying principles of, 212
   using text as external values,
      215–217
Abstract inheritance, 175–176, 179
Acceptance Test-Driven Development (ATDD)

acceptance test framework,
   93–94
acceptance tests, 88
   benefits of, 40
   combining unit tests for auto-
      mated, 39
   connection, 94–95
   creating unit tests from, 40, 44
   defined, 41, 85
   example test, 88–89
   exercise, 95
   flows for development, 85–87
   implementing with FIT, 40
   improving clarity of scope, 42
   no excuses for avoiding, 43
   other advantages, 43
   reducing complexity, 42
   role in continuous integration,
      119–120
   summary review, 96
   testing interface to clarify con-
      tract, 76–77
   user interface for testing, 91–92
   user interface test script, 90–91
   UTDD vs., 42
   what to do if customer won't tell
      you, 95–96
   XUnit testing, 93

M

N

O